COLLECTION OF MASSES OF THE BLESSED VIRGIN MARY

Volume I
MISSAL

COLLECTION OF MASSES OF THE BLESSED VIRGIN MARY

Volume I
MISSAL

APPROVED FOR USE IN THE
DIOCESES OF THE UNITED STATES OF AMERICA
BY THE UNITED STATES CONFERENCE OF CATHOLIC BISHOPS
AND CONFIRMED BY THE APOSTOLIC SEE

Prepared by the
International Commission on English in the Liturgy
A Joint Commission of Catholic Bishops' Conferences
Washington, D.C.
and the
Secretariat of Divine Worship
United States Conference of Catholic Bishops
Washington, D.C.

LITURGICAL PRESS COLLEGEVILLE, MINNESOTA

Concordat cum originali:
✠ Most Reverend Gregory M. Aymond
Chairman, USCCB Committee on Divine Worship
after review by Reverend Monsignor Richard B. Hilgartner
Executive Director, USCCB Secretariat of Divine Worship

Published by authority of the Committee on Divine Worship,
United States Conference of Catholic Bishops

Permission to reprint this ritual with adaptations to conform to *The Roman Missal, Third Edition*, was given by the Congregation for Divine Worship and the Discipline of the Sacraments in a letter dated July 19, 2011 (Prot. n. 692/11/L).

ACKNOWLEDGMENTS

Cover design by Martin Erspamer, OSB, a monk of Saint Meinrad Archabbey.

ISBN 978-0-8146-3486-8

CONTENTS

FOREWORD

Throughout its history the Church has shown a special love and devotion to Mary. The Council of Ephesus bestowed upon the Blessed Virgin her highest and most significant title, *Theotokos*—"God–bearer," that is, Mother of God. Century after century Mary has been praised as being "higher than the cherubim and more glorious than the seraphim" because she said yes to God and through her the Word became flesh and lived among us.

As the Church has reflected on the person and life of Mary, it has come to a deeper realization of what it is to follow Christ. In fact, the early Church saw her as the model—the ideal Christian—who faithfully follows the Lord in word and action. The Second Vatican Council referred to her as the Mother of the Church, since her cooperation in God's plan for the salvation of all helped to make the existence of the Church a reality in this world.

Filled with the Holy Spirit, Mary cried out with joy that "From this day all generations will call me blessed: the Almighty has done great things for me, and holy is his Name." Mary's prophecy has become reality as the Church in the East and the West has glorified God for the humble virgin whom God has exalted for her ever-faithful love.

This collection of Masses in honor of the Blessed Virgin Mary has been a helpful resource as witness to the many ways and reasons Christians have honored Mary. We are happy to re–issue this collection with revisions and adaptations to conform to *The Roman Missal, Third Edition*, so that these Masses will continue to be a source of inspiration and to foster devotion to Mary. Whereever these prayers coincide with prayers in *The Roman Missal, Third Edition,* they were replaced with the new translation. Other adaptations to the language and style of *The Roman Missal* involved the concluding formula of the orations, the Preface dialogue, the introductory formula of the Prefaces, and the Order of Mass. These Masses are a meditation on the history of our salvation in Christ and the very nature of the Christian life. Through the use of this resource of Scripture, prayer, and praise may we join Mary in proclaiming the greatness of the Lord and ever rejoicing in God our Savior.

✠ Gregory M. Aymond
Archbishop of New Orleans
Chairman, Committee on Divine Worship
United States Conference of Catholic Bishops

CONGREGATION FOR DIVINE WORSHIP

Prot. no. 309/86

DECREE

In celebrating the mystery of Christ, the Church also frequently and with deep reverence honors the Blessed Virgin Mary, because of her close bonds with her Son. She is revered by the Church as the new Eve, who, in view of the death of her Son, received at the moment of her conception a higher form of redemption. She is revered as mother, who through the power of the Holy Spirit gave virginal birth to her Son. She is revered as the disciple of Christ, who treasured in her heart the words of Christ the Master. She is revered as the faithful companion of the Redeemer, who, as God had planned, devoted herself with selfless generosity to her Son's mission.

The Church also sees in the Blessed Virgin a preeminent and unique member, graced with all virtue. The Church lovingly cherishes her and never ceases to ask for her protection, for she is the Mother entrusted to us by Christ on the altar of the Cross. The Church proclaims Mary as companion and sister in the journey of faith and in the adversities of life. In Mary, enthroned at Christ's side in the kingdom of heaven, the Church joyfully contemplates the image of its own future glory.

The Fathers of the Second Vatican Ecumenical Council thoroughly reviewed the Church's teaching on the place of the Blessed Virgin Mary within the mystery of Christ and his Church, and also issued principles and norms for the reform of the liturgy. As a consequence, the particular Churches as well as a number of religious institutes have composed new Mass propers. These Masses have been created on the basis of the study of ancient liturgical sources and of the writings of the Fathers of the Church of both the East and the West, on an examination of the documents of the Church's magisterium, and on a judicious balancing of the old and the new. As a result of this work of reform, existing Masses of the Blessed Virgin Mary have been accurately revised and corrected and new Masses composed.

Because of the great number of requests from pastors and the faithful and especially from rectors of Marian shrines, it seemed opportune to publish a collection selected from existing Marian Mass formularies, many of which are outstanding for their teaching, piety, and the significance of their texts. The collection was arranged to cover the cycle of the liturgical year, so that this new organ of the liturgy might foster both in communities and in individuals a genuine devotion toward the Mother of the Lord.

By his apostolic authority Pope John Paul II has approved the *Collectio Missarum de beata Maria Virgine* and has ordered its publication.

Therefore, by special mandate of the Pope, this Congregation for Divine Worship publishes *the Collectio Missarum de beata Maria Virgine*. The Latin text may be used as soon as the book appears. After the Holy See has reviewed the vernacular version, its use will be authorized on the date determined by the Conference of Bishops.

All things to the contrary notwithstanding.

From the office of the Congregation for Divine Worship, 15 August 1986, solemnity of the Assumption of the Blessed Virgin Mary.

Augustin Cardinal Mayer
Prefect

✠ Virgilio Noè
Archbishop of Voncara
Secretary

CONGREGATION FOR DIVINE WORSHIP AND THE DISCIPLINE OF THE SACRAMENTS

Prot. N. 778/89

DECREE

At the request of His Excellency, the Most Reverend Daniel E. Pilarczyk, Archbishop of Cincinnati and President of the National Conference of Catholic Bishops, in a letter dated November 28, 1989, and by virtue of the faculties granted to this Congregation by the Supreme Pontiff, Pope John Paul II, we gladly approve, that is, confirm *ad interim* the English text of the book *Collectio Missarum de Beata Maria Virgine* (Green Book), as it appears in the attached copy.

This decree, by which the requested confirmation is granted by the Apostolic See, is to be included in its entirety in the published text. Two copies of the printed text should be sent to this Congregation.

All things to the contrary notwithstanding.

From the Congregation for Divine Worship and the Discipline of the Sacraments, 20 March 1990.

Eduardo Cardinal Martinez
Prefect

✠ Lajos Kada
Titular Archbishop of Tibica
Secretary

NATIONAL CONFERENCE OF CATHOLIC BISHOPS
UNITED STATES OF AMERICA

DECREE

In accord with the norms established by the decree of the Sacred Congregation of Rites in *Cum, nostra aetate* (27 January 1966), this edition of the *Collection of Masses of the Blessed Virgin Mary* is declared to be the vernacular typical edition of *Collectio Missarum de Beata Maria Virgine* in the dioceses of the United States of America, and is published by authority of the National Conference of Catholic Bishops.

The *Collection of Masses of the Blessed Virgin Mary* was canonically approved for use *ad interim* by the Administrative Committee of the National Conference of Catholic Bishops on 27 September 1989 and was subsequently confirmed by the Apostolic See by decree of the Congregation for Divine Worship on 20 March 1990 (Prot. N. 778/89).

As of 8 September 1992 the *Collection of Masses of the Blessed Virgin Mary* may be published and used in the liturgy. The solemnity of the Immaculate Conception, 8 December 1992, is hereby established as the effective date for the use of the *Collection of Masses of the Blessed Virgin Mary* in the dioceses of the United States of America. From that day forward no other English version may be used.

Given at the General Secretariat of the National Conference of Catholic Bishops, Washington, DC, on 31 May 1992, the feast of the Visitation.

✠ Daniel E. Pilarczyk
Archbishop of Cincinnati
President
National Conference of Catholic Bishops

Robert N. Lynch
General Secretary

GENERAL INTRODUCTION

1 In its presentation of Catholic teaching on the veneration due to Mary as the Mother of Christ, the Second Vatican Council in the Dogmatic Constitution on the Church *Lumen gentium* "counsels all the Church's children to foster wholeheartedly the cultus—especially the liturgical cultus—of the Blessed Virgin:"[1] In the Constitution on the Liturgy *Sacrosanctum Concilium* the Council explains the focus and intent of the universal Church in its liturgical cultus of the Blessed Virgin: "In celebrating the annual cycle of Christ's mysteries, the Church honors with special love Mary, the Mother of God, who is joined by an inseparable bond to the saving work of her Son. In her the Church holds up and admires the most excellent effect of the redemption and joyfully contemplates, as in a flawless image, that which the Church itself desires and hopes wholly to be."[2]

2 Prompted by the call of the Second Vatican Council and guided by the ageold practice and wisdom of the Church, the Apostolic See has gladly devoted its energies to the right promotion of devotion to the Mother of God. Accordingly, in the Roman Liturgy veneration toward the Blessed Virgin Mary is expressed in many wonderful ways, as the General Roman Calendar integrates commemorations of her into the cycle of the liturgical year.[3]

3 Thus on the basis of the arrangement of the Calendar the Roman Liturgy frequently in the course of the year provides the faithful with the opportunity of remembrance of the Blessed Virgin's participation in the mystery of salvation. Clear witnesses to Catholic devotion toward Mary are to be found not only in *The Roman Missal* and *The Liturgy of the Hours*, but also in other liturgical books that contain special celebrations as commemorations to honor the lowly, now glorious Mother of Christ.[4]

I. THE BLESSED VIRGIN MARY IN THE CELEBRATION OF THE MYSTERY OF CHRIST

4 Through its sacred signs the liturgy celebrates the work of salvation that God the Father accomplished through Christ in the Holy Spirit. This salvation is a work that God the Father has carried on through the ages.

---

[1] No. 67: AAS 57 (1965), p. 65; English tr., ICEL, *Documents on the Liturgy*, 1963–1979: *Conciliar, Papal, and Curial Texts*, hereafter DOL (The Liturgical Press, Collegeville, Minn., 1982) 4, no. 161.

[2] Art. 103: AAS 56 (1964), p. 125; DOL 1, no. 103.

[3] Cf. Paul VI, Apostolic Exhortation *Marialis cultus*, no. 2: AAS 66 (1974), p. 117; DOL 467, no. 3900.

[4] Cf., for example, the Roman Ritual, *Book of Blessings* (English edition, 1987), ch. 29, "Order for the Blessing of an Image of the Blessed Virgin Mary," nos. 1004–1017. Cf. also *Order of Crowning an Image of the Blessed Virgin Mary* (English edition, 1986).

This is the salvation announced by the patriarchs and prophets. "The divine plan for the Old Testament was above all arranged so as to prepare, to proclaim in prophecy (cf. Luke 22:44; John 5:39; 1 Peter 1:10), and to prefigure through types (cf. 1 Corinthians 10:11) the coming of Christ, the Redeemer of all, and of his messianic kingdom."[5]

This is the salvation that was fully revealed in Christ Jesus. In the womb of the Virgin of Nazareth, Jesus the Son of God took our human nature and became the Mediator of the Old and the New Covenant. In his Paschal Mystery he brought about our reconciliation with the Father (cf. Colossians 1:22; 2 Corinthians 5:18-19) and through the Spirit of adoption given to us (cf. Romans 8:15-17; Galatians 4:5-6) he joined us closely to himself, so that in spirit and in truth (cf. John 4:23) we might offer worship acceptable to the Father.

This is the salvation that comes to pass in the "age of the Church" through the proclamation of the Gospel and the celebration of the Sacraments (cf. Matthew 28:18-20), which through the centuries make it possible for all to hold fast to the word of salvation and to enter into the Paschal Mystery.

This is the salvation that will reach its consummation in Christ's glorious Second Coming (cf. Matthew 24:30; Acts 1:11), when, having destroyed death, he will subject all things to himself and deliver his kingdom to the Father (cf. 1 Corinthians 15:24-28).

5 When the Church celebrates the sacred mysteries, it celebrates the entire, integral work of salvation. By celebrating things past the Church in a certain sense brings about their presence and in the "mystical today"[6] accomplishes the salvation of the faithful, who as pilgrims through life are in search of that city which is to come (cf. Hebrews 13:14).

Mary, who by the plan of God for the sake of Christ and the Church "was intimately involved in the history of salvation,"[7] was actively present in various, wonderful ways in the mysteries of Christ's life.

6 Masses of the Blessed Virgin Mary have their meaning and purpose from her close participation in the history of salvation. Therefore when the Church commemorates the role of the Mother of the Lord in the work of redemption or honors her privileges, it is above all celebrating the events of salvation in which, by God's salvific plan, the Blessed Virgin was involved in view of the mystery of Christ.

Masses of the Blessed Virgin Mary celebrate the action of God for our salvation

7 Among these events of salvation the Church at the beginning of the liturgical year celebrates the work of God in preparing the Mother of the Redeemer. In her "after the long wait for the fulfill-

[5] Vatican Council II, Dogmatic Constitution on Divine Revelation *Dei Verbum*, no. 15: AAS 58 (1966), p. 825; DOL 14, no. 217.

[6] Cf., for example, *The Liturgy of the Hours*, 25 December, Christmas, Evening Prayer II, antiphon for the Canticle of Mary; 6 January, Epiphany, Evening Prayer II, antiphon for the Canticle of Mary; 2 February, Presentation of the Lord, Evening Prayer II, antiphon for the Canticle of Mary; Ascension, Evening Prayer II, antiphon for the Canticle of Mary.

[7] Vatican Council II, Dogmatic Constitution on the Church *Lumen gentium*, no. 65: AAS 57 (1965), p. 64.

ment of the promise, the time at last came to pass and the new divine economy was established."[8] God came with his grace to Mary and from the first instant of her conception preserved her from all stain of sin, filled her with the gifts of the Holy Spirit, and continued to shelter her with his love, doing great things for her (cf. Luke 1:29) for the sake of our salvation.

8 The Church also celebrates God's intervention in human history in the celebration of the Incarnation of the Word, the birth of Christ and its revelation to the shepherds and the Magi (the first Jewish and the first Gentile converts to the Church, cf. Luke 2:15-16; Matthew 2:1-12), and in the celebration of other events of Christ's infancy. Mary was intimately involved in all of these saving deeds of God. For this reason many of the Mass formularies, a number of which are of great antiquity and liturgical significance, in celebrating the mysteries of Christ's infancy at the same time honor his Mother's part in them.

9 The Church's liturgical celebration of the public life of our Savior, which was marked by the glorious deeds of the Father, is also a commemoration of the Blessed Virgin, "who shared in the mysteries of Christ."[9] For "in Jesus' public life Mary appears on significant occasions. She was present at its beginning, when at the wedding feast of Cana, moved by compassion, she interceded and brought about the first miracle of Jesus the Messiah (cf. John 2:1-11). During his preaching mission, Mary welcomed the words in which her Son extolled the kingdom of God as transcending considerations and bonds of flesh and blood and proclaimed that the truly blessed are those who hear the word of God and keep it (cf. Mark 3:15; Luke 11:27-28), in the way that she herself heard the word of God and faithfully kept it in her heart (cf. Luke 2:19 and 51)."[10]

10 The Church above all celebrates God's wonderful deeds in Christ's Paschal Mystery and in this celebration finds Mary intimately joined to her Son. During his Passion, "she suffered deeply with her Only Begotten Son and, by consenting to his offering himself as Victim, she united her maternal heart to the sacrifice of the one to whom she had given birth."[11] God filled her with joy at the Resurrection of her Son.[12] After Christ's Ascension into heaven, remaining at prayer in the upper room with the Apostles and the first disciples, she implored "the gift of the same Holy Spirit who had come upon her at the moment of the Annunciation."[13]

The presence of Christ in celebrations of the liturgy

11 After Christ's glorious Ascension the work of salvation is carried on above all through celebration of the liturgy, which with good reason may be called the final age in the history of salvation, since in the liturgy Christ is present to the Church in many ways.[14] He is present as the Head of the Mystical Body who presides over the worshiping assembly and whose members are

---

[8] Ibid., no. 55: AAS 57 (1965), p. 60.

[9] Ibid., no. 66: AAS 57 (1965), p. 65; DOL 4, no. 160.

[10] Ibid., no. 58: AAS 57 (1965), p. 61.

[11] Ibid., no. 58: AAS 57 (1965), p. 61.

[12] Cf. *The Liturgy of the Hours*, Common of the Blessed Virgin Mary, Evening Prayer I and II, intercessions, alternate formulary.

[13] Vatican Council II, Dogmatic Constitution on the Church *Lumen gentium*, no. 59: AAS 57 (1965), p. 62.

[14] Cf. Vatican Council II, Constitution on the Liturgy *Sacrosanctum Concilium* (hereafter SC) art. 6–7: AAS 56 (1964), pp. 100–101; DOL 1, nos. 6–7.

marked as a kingly people. He is present as the teacher who continues to proclaim the message of his Gospel. He is present as the Priest who offers the sacrifice of the New Law and who by his power acts in the Sacraments. He is present as the Mediator who without ceasing intercedes for us with the Father (cf. Hebrews 7:25). He is present as the firstborn brother (cf. Romans 8:29) who joins his voice to the voices of his countless brothers and sisters.

The faithful who hold fast to the word of faith and "in the Spirit" take part in the celebration of the liturgy meet the Savior and are joined vitally to the event that brings his salvation.

12 Taken up gloriously into heaven and exalted at the side of her Son, the King of kings and Lord of lords (cf. Revelation 19:16), the Blessed Virgin "did not put aside the saving role given her by God the Father, but by the many ways of her intercession continues to obtain gifts for our eternal salvation."[15] Because of its bonds with Mary, the Church wishes "to live the mystery of Christ"[16] with her and like her and, above all in the liturgy, continually finds that the Blessed Virgin is ever present as the Mother of the Church and its advocate.

13 By its very nature the liturgy wonderfully fosters, effects, and expresses not only the communion existing between the particular Churches throughout the world, but also the communion between the Church on earth and the Angels and Saints in heaven, above all the glorious Mother of God.

Thus in union with the Blessed Virgin[17] and in imitation of her reverent devotion,[18] the Church celebrates the divine mysteries by which "God is perfectly glorified and the participants made holy."[19] The Church joins its voice to Mary's and praises God with her song of thanksgiving.[20] The Church wishes to hear the word of God as she did and to dwell upon it.[21] With Mary it desires to become a sharer in Christ's Paschal Mystery[22] and to join in his redeeming work.[23] In imitation of Mary at prayer in the upper room with the Apostles, the Church ceaselessly implores the gift of the Holy Spirit.[24] The Church invokes her intercession, flies to her protection,[25] prays that she

---

[15] Vatican Council II, Dogmatic Constitution on the Church *Lumen gentium*, no. 62: AAS 57 (1965), p. 63.

[16] Paul VI, Apostolic Exhortation *Marialis cultus*, no. 11: AAS 66 (1974), p. 124; DOL 467, no. 3909.

[17] Cf. *The Roman Missal*, Eucharistic Prayer I (The Roman Canon), "In communion with those whose memory we venerate."

[18] Cf. Paul VI, Apostolic Exhortation *Marialis cultus*, nos. 16–20: AAS 66 (1974), pp. 128–132; DOL 467, nos. 3914–3918.

[19] SC, art. 7: AAS 56 (1964), p. 101; DOL 1, no. 7.

[20] Cf. *The Roman Missal*, 31 May, Visitation, Collect; cf. also Preface II of the Blessed Virgin Mary.

[21] Cf. Roman Ritual, *Book of Blessings*, ch. 4, "Orders for Blessings That Pertain to Catechesis and to Communal Prayer," intercessions, no. 383.

[22] Cf. *The Roman Missal*, 15 September, Our Lady of Sorrows, Collect; Roman Ritual, *Book of Blessings*, ch. 34, "Order for the Blessing of Stations of the Cross," intercessions, no. 1108.

[23] Cf. *The Roman Missal*, Votive Mass of Our Lady, Mother of the Church, Prayer over the Offerings.

[24] Cf. ibid., Preface.

[25] Cf. *Liturgia Horarum*, the Marian antiphon for the end of night prayer *Sub tuum praesidium* (not included in the English translation of the *Liturgia Horarum*).

visit the faithful people and fill them with the gifts of grace,[26] and, under her watchful and gracious gaze upon its progress, goes confidently forward with her to meet Christ.[27]

The power of Mary's example in celebrations of the liturgy

14 The liturgy, which possesses the wonderful power of bringing to mind the realities and events of the past and of making them present here and now, often presents to the faithful the image of the Virgin of Nazareth, who "dedicated herself totally, as handmaid of the Lord, to the person and the work of her Son, serving the mystery of redemption under him and with him."[28]

Thus the Mother of Christ, especially in liturgical services, shines radiantly as the "exemplar of the virtues"[29] and of faithful cooperation in the work of salvation.

15 In doctrine and language deriving from the Fathers of the Church, the liturgy finds many ways to express the power of the Blessed Virgin as exemplar of the Christian life. Particularly when the liturgy seeks to highlight her sanctity and to present her to the faithful as the devoted handmaid of the Father (cf. Luke 1:38; 2:48) and the perfect disciple of Christ, the liturgy calls her the *exemplar*. It calls her a *figure* when it seeks to indicate that her manner of life as virgin, spouse, and mother provides a portrait of the life of the Church and shows the path it must take in its journey of faith and its following of Christ. Finally, the liturgy refers to her as *image*, in order to make it clear that in the Blessed Virgin, who is already perfectly fashioned in the likeness of her Son, the Church "joyfully contemplates, as in a flawless image, that which the Church itself desires and hopes wholly to be."[30]

16 In the liturgy, therefore, the Church invites the faithful to imitate the Blessed Virgin, above all for the faith and obedience with which she lovingly embraced the divine plan of salvation. The hymns and euchological texts of the liturgy unfold the beautiful panoply of virtues in the Mother of Christ that the Church, led by the Holy Spirit, has discovered in its prayer and has learned in its contemplation.

17 The powerful example of Mary that shines out in the celebration of the liturgy urges the faithful to become like the Mother, in order that they might be fashioned more completely in the likeness of her Son. Her example also prompts the faithful to celebrate the mysteries of Christ with that same spirit of reverent devotion with which she took part in the birth of her Son, in his epiphanies, and in his Death and Resurrection. In particular, Mary's example urges the faithful: to treasure the word of God in their hearts and dwell upon it assiduously; to praise God exultantly and thank him joyously; to serve God and neighbor faithfully and offer themselves generously; to pray with perseverance and make their petitions with confidence; to act in all things with mercy and humility; to cherish the law of God and embrace it with love; to love God in everything and above everything else; to be ready to meet Christ when he comes.

---

[26] Cf. *Liturgia Horarum*, 31 May, Visitation, Office of Readings, the hymn *Veni, praecelsa Domina* (not included in the English translation of the *Liturgia Horarum*).

[27] Cf. *The Roman Missal*, Votive Mass of Our Lady, Mother of the Church, Preface.

[28] Vatican Council II, Dogmatic Constitution on the Church *Lumen gentium*, no. 56: AAS 57 (1965), p. 60.

[29] Ibid., no. 65: AAS 57 (1965), p. 64.

[30] SC, art. 103: AAS 56 (1964), p. 125; DOL 1, no. 103. Cf. also *The Roman Missal*, 15 August, Assumption, Preface.

18 In the celebration of Masses of the Blessed Virgin, Priests and all others who have pastoral responsibilities are to strive above all to teach the faithful that the Eucharistic Sacrifice is the memorial of the Death and Resurrection of Christ and to move them to take part in it actively and fully. But Priests and others are not to fail to point out the power of Mary's example that can do so much for the sanctification of the faithful.

II. NATURE OF THE *COLLECTION OF MASSES*

19 The *Collection of Masses of the Blessed Virgin Mary*, approved by Pope John Paul II and promulgated by the Congregation for Divine Worship, has a specific purpose with regard to the *cultus* of the Blessed Virgin Mary. The Collection seeks to promote celebrations that are marked by sound doctrine, the rich variety of their themes, and their rightful commemoration of the saving deeds that the Lord God has accomplished in the Blessed Virgin in view of the mystery of Christ and the Church.

20 The *Collection of Masses* is made up principally of the texts for Marian Masses that are found in the propers of the particular Churches or of religious institutes or in *The Roman Missal*.

21 The *Collection of Masses* is intended for:

Marian shrines where Masses of the Blessed Virgin Mary are celebrated frequently, in accord with the provisions to be indicated in nos. 29–33;

ecclesial communities that on the Saturdays in Ordinary Time desire to celebrate a Mass of the Blessed Virgin, in accord with the provision to be indicated in no. 34.

As will be pointed out in no. 37, use of the *Collection* of Masses is permitted on days on which, according to the *General Instruction of the Roman Missal*, the Priest is free to choose which Mass he will celebrate.[31]

22 Promulgation of the *Collection of Masses of the Blessed Virgin Mary* introduces no change in the General Roman Calendar, issued 21 March 1969, in *The Roman Missal*, second *editio typica*, issued 27 March 1975, in the *Lectionary for Mass*, second *editio typica*, issued 21 January 1981, or in the system of rubrics currently in force.

III. STRUCTURE OF THE *COLLECTION OF MASSES*

23 Within the cycle of a year the Church in an orderly pattern unfolds the whole mystery of Christ. This mystery begins with the eternal plan of predestination, in which Christ, the Word made flesh, stands as principle and head, as end and fulfillment of the human race and of all creation; it extends to his glorious Second Coming, when all things will be brought to completion in him, "that God may be all in all (1 Corinthians 15:28)."[32]

---

[31] *General Instruction of the Roman Missal*, hereafter GIRM, no. 355 c).

[32] Cf. SC, art 102: AAS 56 (1964), p. 125; DOL 1, no. 102. Cf. also *Universal Norms on the Liturgical Year and the Calendar*, ch. 1, no. 1: DOL 442, no. 3767.

24 Since Mary is so closely linked with the mystery of Christ, the *Collection of Masses of the Blessed Virgin Mary* is arranged in accord with the divisions of the liturgical year. With the mystery celebrated as the primary criterion, therefore, the forty-six formularies in the *Collection of Masses* are distributed over the seasons of the liturgical year: Advent (three formularies), Christmas Time (six formularies), Lent (five formularies), Easter Time (four formularies), Ordinary Time (twenty-eight formularies).

The formularies for Ordinary Time are divided into three sections. The first section contains eleven formularies for celebrations of the Mother of God under titles that are derived chiefly from Sacred Scripture or that express Mary's bond with the Church. The second section contains nine formularies to honor the memory of the Blessed Virgin Mary under titles that refer to her cooperation in fostering the spiritual life of the faithful. The third section contains eight formularies to celebrate the memory of the Blessed Virgin under titles that suggest her compassionate intercession on behalf of the faithful.

As a result of this arrangement of Masses, the occasions and manner of Mary's cooperation in the work of salvation will be celebrated and in the most appropriate liturgical season; in addition the Blessed Virgin's close connection with the mission of the Church will be clearly expressed.

25 In accord with the practice of the Roman Liturgy the *Collection of Masses* is made up of two volumes.

> The first contains the euchological texts, the Entrance and Communion Antiphons, and, in an appendix, several formularies for Solemn Blessings at the end of Mass.

The second volume contains the biblical readings assigned for each Mass, together with the Responsorial Psalms and the *Alleluia* verse or verse before the Gospel reading.

26 In Volume 1 a historical, liturgical, and pastoral introduction precedes each formulary, in order to assist the preparation for the Eucharistic celebration. Each brief introduction indicates the origin of the memorial or title of the Blessed Virgin, provides, in some cases, the sources of the formulary, and explains its teaching, which is based on biblical and euchological texts.

IV. USE OF THE COLLECTION OF MASSES

27 If the *Collection of Masses of the Blessed Virgin Mary* is to achieve the objective intended, it must be used properly everywhere and by all.

Observance of the seasons of the liturgical year

28 For the correct use of the *Collection of Masses* the Priest Celebrant must respect the seasons of the liturgical year. As a rule, therefore, the Mass formularies are to be used during the liturgical season to which they have been assigned. But for a just reason certain formularies may be used in some other liturgical season. For example:

> The Mass, "Our Lady of Nazareth," which is included among the Masses for Christmas Time (no. 8), may rightly be celebrated during Ordinary Time when a group of the faithful wish to commemorate the life led by the Virgin of Nazareth and the power of its example.

The Mass, "The Blessed Virgin Mary, Mother of Reconciliation," which is included among the formularies assigned to the season of Lent (no. 14), may also be properly used during Ordinary Time, when the Eucharist is celebrated for the purpose of arousing a spirit of reconciliation and concord.

On the other hand such Masses as the Mass, "The Blessed Virgin Mary and the Epiphany of the Lord" (no. 6) or the Mass, "The Blessed Virgin Mary and the Resurrection of the Lord" (no. 15), may not be celebrated outside the seasons to which they have been assigned, because of their specific congruence with these seasons.

A. Use of the "Collection of Masses" in Marian sanctuaries

29 As indicated already in no. 21, the *Collection of Masses of the Blessed Virgin Mary* is intended first of all for use in Marian shrines, in order to foster authentic devotion to the Virgin at these shrines and to suffuse it with the true spirit of the liturgy.

This purpose will be of great advantage for the particular Churches, since their pastoral concerns are to such a great extent sustained and nurtured by the initiatives and programs carried out in shrines dedicated to the Blessed Virgin. As the *Code of Canon Law* directs, "at shrines more abundant means of salvation are to be provided the faithful; the word of God is to be carefully proclaimed; liturgical life is to be appropriately fostered, especially through the celebration of the Eucharist and Penance; and approved forms of popular piety are to be cultivated."[33]

30 Celebration of the Eucharist is the high point and center of all pastoral activity at a shrine. Participation in the Eucharistic celebration is the principal intent of large pilgrimages of the faithful to a shrine, or of groups that meet there for study or prayer, or of individuals who go there to implore some special favor of God or for quiet contemplation.

In accord with the individual circumstances of the faithful or groups of the faithful, then, every measure is to be taken to ensure that the liturgy is celebrated in an exemplary way and that in its celebration of the divine mysteries the worshiping community will itself become the faithful image of the Church.[34]

31 Accordingly, it has been the practice of the Congregation for Divine Worship to grant permission to Marian shrines for a more frequent celebration of Masses of the Blessed Virgin Mary.

The following norms are to be observed in the use of the *Collection of Masses of the Blessed Virgin Mary*.

a) As long as the liturgical season is respected, the Masses provided in the *Collection of Masses* may be celebrated on any day except those listed in nos. 1–6 of the Table of Liturgical Days.[35]

---

[33] *Code of Canon Law*, can. 1234.

[34] Cf. SC, art. 2: AAS 56 (1964), pp. 97–98; DOL 1, no. 2.

[35] In the *Universal Norms on the Liturgical Year and the Calendar*, no. 59 (DOL 442, no. 3825), Table of Liturgical Days, nos. 1–6 are as follows:

1. The Paschal Triduum of the Passion and Resurrection of the Lord.
2. The Nativity of the Lord, the Epiphany, the Ascension, and Pentecost.

b) The permission stated in paragraph a) is granted only for the Priests who are part of a pilgrimage or for Priests who celebrate Mass for the benefit of the members of a pilgrimage.

c) During the seasons of Advent, Christmas, Lent, and Easter, the biblical readings are to be those assigned in the *Lectionary for Mass* for each day of the particular season except in the case of a celebration in the manner of a Feast or Solemnity.

"Proper Mass" of a shrine

32 Because of the relevance of the texts of the "proper Mass" of a shrine to the title under which the Blessed Virgin is honored there, the Priests and faithful on pilgrimage usually wish to celebrate that Mass.

But care must be taken to respect the different liturgical seasons, so that the "proper Mass" of a shrine is not the only Mass celebrated there. Rather the Mass formularies are to be intelligently varied, so that the celebration of the Eucharist provides the faithful with an overview of the entire history of salvation and of the bonds that have joined Mary to the mystery of Christ and the Church.

33 The following is an indication, by way of example, of circumstances in which the formularies of the *Collection of Masses* may opportunely replace the "proper Mass" of a shrine:

a. during the seasons of Advent, Christmas, Lent, and Easter, when the formularies provided in the *Collection of Masses* are so perfectly relevant to the mystery of Christ then being celebrated;

b. during a pilgrimage that is to spend a number of days at a shrine or that is made up of pilgrims who visit the shrine frequently.

B. Use of the "Collection of Masses" for a memorial of the Blessed Virgin on Saturday

34 As already mentioned in no. 21, the *Collection of Masses of the Blessed Virgin Mary* is also intended for ecclesial communities that "on Saturdays in Ordinary Time when no Obligatory

---

Sundays of Advent, Lent, and Easter.
Ash Wednesday.
Weekdays of Holy Week from Monday up to and including Thursday.
Days within the Octave of Easter.

3. Solemnities inscribed in the General Calendar, whether of the Lord, of the Blessed Virgin Mary, or of Saints. The Commemoration of All the Faithful Departed.

4. Proper Solemnities, namely:
   a) The Solemnity of the principal Patron of the place, the city or state.
   b) The Solemnity of the dedication and of the anniversary of the dedication of one's own church.
   c) The Solemnity of the Title of one's own church.

Memorial occurs"[36] often celebrate a memorial of the Blessed Virgin and therefore wish to have available a number of Mass formularies.

35 The custom of dedicating Saturday to the Blessed Virgin Mary arose in Carolingian monasteries at the end of the eighth century and soon spread throughout Europe.[37] The custom also was incorporated into liturgical books of the particular Churches and became part of the heritage of the religious orders of evangelical and apostolic life that were founded early in the thirteenth century.

In the liturgical reform following the Council of Trent, the custom of celebrating a memorial of the Blessed Virgin Mary on Saturday was incorporated into the *Missale Romanum.*

The liturgical reform initiated by the Second Vatican Council clarified the meaning of the memorial of the Blessed Virgin on Saturday and gave it new vigor by making possible a more frequent celebration of this memorial, increasing the number of formularies and biblical readings, and revising the euchological texts.

36 A number of ecclesial communities celebrate the memorial of the Blessed Virgin on Saturday as a kind of introduction to the Lord's Day. As they prepare to celebrate the weekly remembrance of the Lord's Resurrection, these communities look with great reverence to the Blessed Virgin, who, alone of all his disciples, on that "great Sabbath" when Christ lay in the tomb, kept watch with full faith and hope and awaited his resurrection.[38]

This "ancient and . . . , as it were, humble memorial"[39] of Mary recurring each week is in a certain way a reminder of the unfailing presence of the Blessed Virgin in the life of the Church.

C. Use of the "Collection of Masses" on days when Masses ad libitum may be celebrated

37 On days when, according to the *General Instruction of the Roman Missal*, the choice of Masses is left open,[40] a Priest celebrating Mass, whether with or without a congregation, has the option of using one of the formularies in the *Collection of Masses*. But "the first concern of a Priest celebrating with a congregation is the spiritual benefit of the faithful and he will be careful not to impose his personal preference on them. Above all he will make sure not to omit too often or without suf-

---

d) The Solemnity either of the Title
or of the Founder
or of the principal Patron of an Order or Congregation.

5. Feasts of the Lord inscribed in the General Calendar.

6. Sundays of Christmas Time and the Sundays in Ordinary Time.

[36] *Universal Norms on the Liturgical Year and the Calendar*, no. 15: DOL 442, no. 3781.

[37] Cf. Bernold of Constance, *Micrologus de ecclesiasticis observationibus*, ch. 60: PL 151, 1020.

[38] Cf. Humbert of Romans, *De vita regulari*, ch. 24, "Why Saturday is the day assigned to the Blessed Virgin": vol. 2 (A. Befani, Rome, 1889), pp. 72–73.

[39] Paul VI, Apostolic Exhortation *Marialis cultus*, no. 9: AAS 66 (1974), p. 122; DOL 467, no. 3907.

[40] GIRM, no. 355 c).

ficient cause the readings assigned for each day in the weekday Lectionary; the Church's desire is that a more lavish table of the word of God be spread before the faithful."[41]

Priests and faithful should keep in mind that genuine Marian devotion does not demand the multiplication of Masses of the Blessed Virgin, but that in their celebration everything—readings, songs, homily, Universal Prayer, the offering of the sacrifice—be done with propriety, care, and a vital liturgical spirit.

V. THE WORD OF GOD IN THE FORMULARIES OF THE *COLLECTION OF MASSES*

38 The particular objective of every liturgical memorial is expressed and defined through both its euchological texts and its biblical readings. It is therefore clear why even from the earliest times the greatest care has been taken in the choosing of passages of Scripture. It is also clear why each formulary in the *Collection of Masses* has been assigned its own plan of readings for the celebration of the word of God.

39 The biblical readings of the *Collection of Masses of the Blessed Virgin Mary* constitute a rich and varied corpus that in the course of the centuries has been created by the ecclesial communities of both the past and the present.

Within this biblical corpus it is possible to distinguish three types of readings:

a. readings from both the Old and the New Testament that relate to the life or mission of the Blessed Virgin or that contain prophecies about her;

b. readings from the Old Testament that from antiquity have been applied to Mary. The Fathers of the Church have always regarded the Sacred Scriptures of both the Old and the New Covenant as a single corpus that is permeated by the mystery of Christ. Accordingly certain events, figures, or symbols of the Old Testament foretell or suggest in a wonderful manner the life and mission of the Blessed Virgin Mary, the glorious daughter of Zion and Mother of Christ;

c. readings of the New Testament that, while not referring to the Blessed Virgin, still are assigned to the celebration of her memorial in order to make clear that all the virtues extolled in the Gospel, faith, charity, hope, humility, mercy, purity of heart flourished in Mary, the first and most perfect of Christ's disciples.

40 The following points are to be noted with regard to the readings assigned to each formulary in the *Collection of Masses*.

a. Only two readings are provided; the first is from the Old Testament, from an Apostle (that is, from the Epistles or from Revelation) or, in Easter Time, from Acts or Revelation; the second reading is from one of the Gospels.

---

[41] *Lectionary for Mass* (2nd *editio typica*, 1981), General Introduction, no. 83; cf. also GIRM, no. 355c. SC, art. 51: AAS 56 (1964), p. 114; DOL 1, no. 51.

b. But in special, more solemn celebrations when the Priest and the faithful wish to have three readings proclaimed at Mass, the additional reading is taken from the texts provided in the *Lectionary for Mass*, the Common of the Blessed Virgin Mary, or from the texts contained in the appendix of the Lectionary for the *Collection of Masses*. The provisions of the *Lectionary for Mass*, General Introduction, nos. 78–81 ("Principles to Be Followed in the Use of the Order of Readings), are to be observed.

c. The readings that are indicated in the *Collection of Masses* for each Mass formulary will be most appropriate for the celebration of some special memorial of the Blessed Virgin. Still, celebrants have the option of replacing these readings with other appropriate readings, taken at will from those contained in *the Lectionary for Mass*, Common of the Blessed Virgin Mary, or in the appendix of the Lectionary for the *Collection of Masses*.[42]

41 The following are to be observed with regard to the liturgy of the word.

a. During the seasons of Advent, Christmas, Lent, and Easter (except for the concession in no. 31 c), the readings are to be those assigned in the seasonal *Lectionary for Mass* for each day of these seasons, lest the "continuous reading" of Scripture be interrupted or readings that express the particular character of a season be neglected.

b. During Ordinary Time it is up to the Priest Celebrant "in harmony with those who exercise some part in the celebration, including the faithful,"[43] to decide which is more beneficial: to take the readings from the *Collection of Masses* or to take them from the seasonal *Lectionary for Mass*.

VI. ADAPTATIONS

42 It belongs to the Conference of Bishops to see to the vernacular translation of the *Collection of Masses*, in accord with the existing norms provided for such translations,[44] so as to ensure that the translation is consonant with the idiom of the various languages and the genius of the various cultures. Whenever opportune, melodies suitable for singing should be added to the translation.

43 It also belongs to the Conference of Bishops to include as an appendix to the vernacular edition previously approved formularies for Masses of the Blessed Virgin Mary under titles by which she is venerated by the faithful of an entire nation or region or of a large section of the nation or region.

---

[42] Cf. *Lectionary for Mass* (2nd *editio typica*, 1981), Common of the Blessed Virgin Mary, nos. 707–712; cf. also vol. 2 of the *Collection of Masses*, Appendix, nos. 1–21.

[43] GIRM, no. 352. Cf. *Lectionary for Mass* (2nd *editio typica*, 1981), General Introduction, no. 78.

[44] Cf. Consilium for the Carrying Out of the Constitution on the Liturgy, Instruction on the translation of liturgical texts for celebrations with a congregation, 25 January 1969: *Notitiae 5* (1969), pp. 3–12; DOL 123, nos. 838–880. Congregation for the Sacraments and Divine Worship, Circular Letter to presidents of the conferences of bishops, on the use of the vernacular in the liturgy, 5 June 1976: *Notitiae* 12 (1976), pp. 300–302; DOL 133, nos. 911–917.

SIGLA

Documents of Vatican II and Papal Documents

LG	Dogmatic Constitution on the Church *Lumen gentium*
MC	Apostolic Exhortation *Marialis Cultus*, on rightly grounding and increasing Marian devotion
SC	Constitution on the Sacred Liturgy *Sacrosanctum Concilium*

Bibliographical Abbreviations

AAS	*Acta Apostolicae Sedis. Commentarium officiale* (Vatican City, 1909–)
ASS	*Acta Sanctae Sedis. Ephemerides Romanae. Authenticae et officiales* (Rome, 1865–1908)
CSEL	*Corpus scriptorum ecclesiasticorum Latinorum* (Vienna, 1866–)
LH	*Liturgia Horarum*
MR	*Missale Romanum, editio typica tertia emendata* (2008)
OLM	*Ordo Lectionum Missae*
Pa	*Sacramentarium Paduense* (The Sacramentary of Padua)
PG	*Patrologiae cursus completus: Series graeca*, J.P. Migne, ed., 161 v. (Paris, 1857–66)
PL	*Patrologiae cursus completus: Series latina*, J.P. Migne, ed., 222 v. (Paris, 1844–55)
Sch	*Sources chrétiennes*, H. de Lubac et al., ed. (Paris, 1941–)
Ve	*Sacramentarium Veronense* (The Verona Sacramentary)

Abbreviations for the Identification of Texts

All	*Alleluia*
Ant	Antiphon
Col	Collect
Com Ant	Communion Antiphon
Ent Ant	Entrance Antiphon
Gos	Gospel Reading
Gos Ver	Gospel Verse
1 Read	First Reading
PC	Prayer after Communion
PO	Prayer over the Offerings
Pref	Preface
Resp	Responsorial Psalm

ADVENT

During Advent the Roman Liturgy celebrates the two comings of the Lord: the First Coming in lowliness, when in the fullness of time (cf. Galatians 4:4) the Lord took flesh of the Blessed Virgin Mary and came into the world to save the human race; the Second Coming in glory, when at the end of time the Lord will come "to judge the living and the dead" *(Creed)* and to lead the just into the house of his Father where Mary has preceded them in glory.

MASS FORMULARIES

1. The Blessed Virgin Mary, Chosen Daughter of Israel
2. The Blessed Virgin Mary and the Annunciation of the Lord
3. The Visitation of the Blessed Virgin Mary

1. THE BLESSED VIRGIN MARY, CHOSEN DAUGHTER OF ISRAEL

During Advent the Roman Liturgy celebrates the plan of salvation by which the merciful God called the patriarchs, united them to himself in a covenant of love, established the Law through Moses, raised up the prophets, and chose David as the one from whose line the Savior of the world was to be born. The books of the Old Testament, in foretelling the coming of Christ, "gradually bring into clearer light the figure of a woman, the Mother of the Redeemer" (LG, n. 55): she is the Blessed Virgin Mary, whom the Church proclaims as the joy of Israel and the noble daughter of Zion.

Our Lady, who undid the sin of Eve by her sinlessness, "is by nature the daughter of Adam" (Pref; in believing the message of the angel she conceived the Son of God in her virginal womb: "she is by faith the true child of Abraham" (Pref); "she is by descent the branch from the root of Jesse, bearing the flower that is Jesus Christ our Lord" (Pref).

In her sincere obedience to the Law and her wholehearted acceptance of God's will, she is, in the words of the Second Vatican Council, "exalted among the humble and poor of the Lord, who trustingly hope in him for salvation and from him receive it. After the long period of waiting for the fulfillment of the promise, in her at last the fullness of time is reached, and a new order of providence is begun, when the Son of God takes from her a human nature in order to free the human family from sin through the mysteries of his earthly life" (LG, no. 55).

This Mass in honor of our Lady, chosen daughter of Israel, recalls and celebrates this mystery of God's mercy and our salvation.

The first reading appropriately commemorates either God's promise to Abraham ("All the communities of the earth shall find blessing in you": 1 Read, Genesis 12:1-7; cf. Luke 1:55) or God's promise to David through the prophet Nathan ("Your house and your kingdom shall endure forever before me; your throne shall stand firm forever": 1 Read, 2 Samuel 7:1-5, 8b-11, 16; cf. Luke 1:32-33). The Gospel reading proclaims the ancestry of Christ (Gos, Matthew 1:1-17), showing that our Savior is son of David and son of Abraham (cf. Matthew 1:1).

Entrance Antiphon Cf. Zephaniah 3:14; Haggai 2:8

Rejoice and be glad with all your heart, daughter of Jerusalem;
the Desired of all nations is coming,
and the house of the Lord will be filled with glory.

COLLECT

A O God, who chose the Blessed Virgin Mary,
foremost among the poor and humble,
to be the Mother of the Savior,
grant, we pray, that, following her example,
we may offer you the homage of sincere faith
and place in you all our hope of salvation.
Through our Lord Jesus Christ, your Son,
who lives and reigns with you in the unity of the Holy Spirit,
God, for ever and ever.

B O God, who, fulfilling the promise made to our Fathers,
chose the Blessed Virgin Mary,
the noble daughter of Zion,
grant that we may follow her example,
for her humility was pleasing to you
and her obedience profitable to us.
Through our Lord Jesus Christ, your Son,
who lives and reigns with you in the unity of the Holy Spirit,
God, for ever and ever.

PRAYER OVER THE OFFERINGS

Accept, O Lord, these offerings,
and by your power change them into the Sacrament of salvation,
in which, fulfilling the sacrifices of the Fathers,
is offered the true Lamb, Jesus Christ your Son,
born of the ever-Virgin Mary in a way beyond all telling.
Who lives and reigns for ever and ever.

Preface P 1, page 80.

Communion Antiphon

Rejoice and be glad, O joy of Israel!
Through the angel you received the world's joy!
Rejoice and be glad, for you brought to birth for us the Bread of Life!

PRAYER AFTER COMMUNION

Refreshed, Lord God, by this life-giving Sacrament,
we call out to you and pray
that as we see in Christ, born of the Virgin,
the promise to Israel fulfilled,
so in his Second Coming we may attain
the joyful fulfillment of all our hope.
Through Christ our Lord.

2. THE BLESSED VIRGIN MARY AND THE ANNUNCIATION OF THE LORD

During Advent the liturgy reminds us every day of the message of Gabriel to our Lady: "The angel Gabriel said to Mary in greeting: Hail, full of grace, the Lord is with you; blessed are you among women" (Ant at Midday Prayer), and prays each day: "Loving Mother of the Redeemer, . . . you who received Gabriel's joyful greeting: have pity on us poor sinners" (Final Ant).

The consent of our Lady, which in God's good pleasure preceded the Incarnation (cf. LG, no. 56), is of the greatest importance in the story of salvation, for the Incarnation of the Word is the restoration of human nature.

The Roman Liturgy recalls this Sacrament of our salvation, not only on the Solemnity of 25 March but also, as the Nativity of the Lord approaches, on 20 December and particularly on the Fourth Sunday of Advent in Year B; the celebration of this mystery fits in admirably with the character and nature of the Advent.

For this reason the Mass of the Blessed Virgin Mary and the Annunciation of the Lord is very suitably used whenever, for a good reason, during Advent a memorial of the Mother of the Lord is to be celebrated.

In such celebrations the Mass readings are taken from the prophecy of the virgin who is to give birth ("the virgin shall conceive and bear a son": 1 Read, Isaiah 7:10-14; 8:10c) and the message of Gabriel to the Virgin of Nazareth: ("Behold, you will conceive in your womb and bear a son": Gos, Luke 1:26-38).

This Mass was formerly celebrated on the Ember Days of Advent. Because of its beauty it was frequently known in the Middle Ages as "the Golden Mass."

The formulary is to be found in *The Roman Missal*, in the Common of the Blessed Virgin Mary during Advent, except for the Prayer over the Offerings, which is taken from the Fourth Sunday of Advent, and the Preface, which is taken from the Mass of the Solemnity of the Annunciation of the Lord on 25 March.

Entrance Antiphon

A Drop down dew from above, you heavens, Cf. Isaiah 45:8
and let the clouds rain down the Just One;
let the earth be opened and bring forth a Savior.

B The angel said to Mary: You have found favor with God. Luke 1:30-32
Behold, you will conceive and bear a son,
and he will be called Son of the Most High.

COLLECT

O God, who willed that at the message of an Angel
your Word should take flesh
in the womb of the Blessed Virgin Mary,
grant that we, who pray to you
and believe her to be truly the Mother of God
may be helped by her interceding before you.
Through our Lord Jesus Christ, your Son,
who lives and reigns with you in the unity of the Holy Spirit,
God, for ever and ever.

PRAYER OVER THE OFFERINGS

May the Holy Spirit, O Lord,
sanctify these gifts laid upon your altar,
just as he filled with his power
the womb of the Blessed Virgin Mary.
Through Christ our Lord.

Preface P 2, page 81.

Communion Antiphon Cf. Isaiah 7:14

Behold, a Virgin shall conceive and bear a son;
and his name will be called Emmanuel.

PRAYER AFTER COMMUNION

May the mysteries we have received,
O Lord our God,
always show forth your mercy in us,
that we, who honor the Mother of your Son
may be saved by his incarnation.
Who lives and reigns for ever and ever.

3. THE VISITATION OF THE BLESSED VIRGIN MARY

On more than one occasion the Roman Liturgy celebrates the grace-filled mystery in the unfolding of salvation when the Virgin Mary, overshadowed by the Holy Spirit and bearing the Word of God, visits Elizabeth: on the Feast itself (31 May), before the Solemnity of the Nativity of Saint John the Baptist (24 June); during Advent, because of its close connection with the Solemnity of Christmas, on 21 December; and in particular on the Fourth Sunday of Advent of Year C.

The Mass of the Visitation of the Blessed Virgin Mary is appropriate during Advent when a memorial of the Mother of the Lord is to be celebrated for a reasonable cause.

Our Lady in visiting her kinswoman Elizabeth is an image of the mystery of salvation, in which God "has come to his people and set them free" (Ent Ant, Luke 1:68). Mary is also the model for the Church, which God nourishes with his gifts and on which he pours out his Holy Spirit (cf. PC) as it brings the message of joy to the whole world so that all peoples may "acknowledge Christ as their Savior" (PC).

In this Mass our Lady is honored as:

—*the new daughter of Zion*, who in her womb ("in your midst") bears the Lord, the King of Israel (1 Read, Zephaniah 3:14-18a);

—*the new ark of the covenant*, who, bearing the Word of God, brings "salvation and joy to the home of Elizabeth" (Col, cf. 1 Chronicles 13:14);

—*a new creation*, formed by the Holy Spirit (cf. PO and LG, no. 56), who is bathed in the dew of heavenly grace (cf. PO), and bears the fruit of salvation, Jesus Christ;

—*the Mother of the Lord*, whom Elizabeth recognizes in words inspired by the Holy Spirit (cf. Pref) and who gives herself completely to the mystery of redemption;

—*a holy woman*, who, hearing the words of an angel, hastens to play her part in the work of salvation, proclaims God's greatness in her song of praise and thanksgiving (cf. Gos, Luke 1:39-56); a paragon of loving service (cf. Pref), she is rightly hailed as blessed "because she believed in your [God's] promise of salvation" (Pref, cf. *All*, Luke 1:45), whose humility is looked upon with favor by God (cf. Com Ant, Luke 1:48) and will be acclaimed by all generations.

Entrance Antiphon Luke 1:68-69a, 70

Blessed be the Lord, the God of Israel;
he has come to his people and set them free.
He has raised up for us a mighty savior,
as his holy prophets promised of old.

COLLECT

Lord our God, Savior of the human family,
you brought salvation and joy
to the home of Elizabeth
through the visit of the Blessed Virgin Mary,
the ark of the New Covenant.
We ask that, in obedience
to the inspiration of the Holy Spirit,
we too may bring Christ to others
and proclaim your greatness
by the praise of our lips and the holiness of our lives.
Through our Lord Jesus Christ, your Son,
who lives and reigns with you in the unity of the Holy Spirit,
God, for ever and ever.

PRAYER OVER THE OFFERINGS

Lord,
may our gifts be sanctified by the Holy Spirit,
who formed the Blessed Virgin Mary
to be a new creation,
and bathed her with the dew of heavenly grace,
so that she might bear the fruit of salvation.
Through Christ our Lord.

Preface P 3, page 82.

Communion Antiphon Luke 1:48

The Lord has looked on his lowly handmaid;
behold, henceforth all all generations will call me blessed.

PRAYER AFTER COMMUNION

Lord our God,
you have nourished the Church with your sacramental gifts
and poured out on it your Holy Spirit;
may it hasten to bring your message of joy to the whole world,
so that all peoples who receive your saving word
may rejoice in your redeeming love
and acknowledge Christ as their Savior.
Who lives and reigns for ever and ever.

CHRISTMAS TIME

During Christmas Time the Church celebrates the mysteries of the childhood of Christ the Savior and his first manifestations. For this reason this liturgical period, though it ends with the Feast of the Baptism of the Lord, nevertheless includes the Mass of the Lord's manifestation at the wedding feast of Cana.

In the divine plan the Blessed Virgin was involved in many wonderful ways in the mysteries of the Savior's childhood and manifestations. By a virginal birth she brought forth the Son, showed him to the shepherds and the magi, presented him in the temple and offered him to the Lord. She took her child into exile in Egypt, searched for him when he was lost, and in the home of Nazareth she and Joseph, her husband, led their holy and busy life with Christ. At the wedding feast of Cana she asked a favor of her Son on behalf of the bride and groom and Jesus performed the first "of his signs . . . and so revealed his glory" (John 2:11).

MASS FORMULARIES

4. Holy Mary, Mother of God
5. The Blessed Virgin Mary, Mother of the Savior
6. The Blessed Virgin Mary and the Epiphany of the Lord
7. The Blessed Virgin Mary and the Presentation of the Lord
8. Our Lady of Nazareth
9. Our Lady of Cana

4. HOLY MARY, MOTHER OF GOD

This Mass celebrates the "wonderful and inexpressible mystery" (Pref), by which the Father of mercies sent his Son "from heaven into the womb of the Blessed Virgin" (Col, A; cf. St. Hippolytus, *Traditio apostolica*, 4: Sch, 11 bis, p. 48) to be "[his] saving Word and our Bread of Life" (Col, A). It also commemorates both the faith and the humility with which our Lady "conceived your only Son and bore [him] in her pure womb" (Pref). The humble Virgin of Nazareth is thus set before us as an example: like her we are to receive the Son of God by "treasuring his words in our hearts and celebrating with deep faith the mysteries of our redemption" (Col, A), to reveal him in the holiness of our lives (cf. Col, B), "profess him in words and hold fast to him in deeds" (PC).

The texts of this Mass echo the writings of the Fathers of the Church and ancient liturgical prayers, and in particular:

—the thought of St. Augustine (d. 430) that our Lady "conceived him [Christ] in her heart before she conceived him in her womb" (Col, B; *Sermo* 25, 7: PL 38, 937); Augustine praises her faith and obedience and sets before us her spiritual relationship with her Son;

—the saying of St. Bernard (d. 1153) that though our Lady was pleasing to God because of her virginity, yet it was through her humility that she conceived him (cf. *In laudibus Virginis Matris*, I, 5: *Opera omnia*, IV, ed. Cistercienses, Rome, 1966, p. 18).

The Preface should be noted: it admirably extols the virginal and salvific motherhood of our Lady: "What joy is hers at [God's] twofold gift: she is full of wonder at her virgin-motherhood and full of joy at giving birth to the Redeemer." Experts in liturgy rank this among the oldest Prefaces in honor of our Lady: it is found in the *Sacramentarium Paduense* (Pa, 387).

Entrance Antiphon

A O Virgin Mother of God,
he whom the whole world cannot contain
cloistered himself within your womb, made man for us.

B Hail, Holy Mother, who gave birth to the King
who rules heaven and earth for ever.

COLLECT

A Lord our God,
you sent your Son from heaven
into the womb of the Blessed Virgin
to be your saving Word and our Bread of Life.
Grant that like Mary we may welcome Christ
by treasuring his words in our hearts
and celebrating with deep faith
the mysteries of our redemption.
Through our Lord Jesus Christ, your Son,
who lives and reigns with you in the unity of the Holy Spirit,
God, for ever and ever.

B Lord God,
when your Son came down from heaven
Mary conceived him in her heart
before she conceived him in her womb.
Grant that by holy and just deeds
we may show forth in our lives
the Christ, whom we have received by faith.
Who lives and reigns with you in the unity of Holy Spirit,
God, for ever and ever.

PRAYER OVER THE OFFERINGS

May the offerings your people make
on this memorial of the Blessed Virgin Mary
be acceptable to you, O Lord,
for by her virginity she pleased you
and in humility conceived your Son, our Lord.
Who lives and reigns for ever and ever.

Preface P 4, page 83.

Communion Antiphon

Blessed is the womb of the Virgin Mary,
which bore the Son of the eternal Father.

PRAYER AFTER COMMUNION

Renewed with this heavenly food,
we humbly implore you, Lord,
that having received your Son, born of the tender Virgin,
under sacramental signs,
we may profess him in words
and hold fast to him in deeds.
Who lives and reigns for ever and ever.

5. THE BLESSED VIRGIN MARY, MOTHER OF THE SAVIOR

This Mass of the Blessed Virgin Mary, Mother of the Savior, is found in *The Roman Missal* in the Common of the Blessed Virgin Mary, Christmas Time. Its texts are both ancient and full of beauty. The Preface is taken from the venerable *Sacramentarium Veronense* (Ve 1247).

This Mass, resounding with Christmas joy and light, celebrates:

—above all, the maternal role of our Lady in relation to her Son, acknowledged as the King "whose name is eternal" (Ent Ant), as the Son of God (cf. Col, Pref, PC), as the "author of life" (Col, cf. Acts 3:15), as the "sign and source of our salvation" (Pref), as "a light for all nations" (Pref, cf. Luke 2:32), as "the Bridegroom" (Pref, cf. Psalm 19:6), and as the Word made flesh (cf. Com Ant, cf. John 1:14);

—the fruitful virginity of our Lady (cf. Col) and her virgin-motherhood, by means of which God gave to the human race the gift of "eternal salvation" (Col), as well as the marvelous way in which "a mother's joy" coexists in her with "a virgin's honor" (Ent Ant); this motherhood is the source of her unique status and dignity, for "none like her was seen before and none thereafter" (Ent Ant);

—the unceasing intercession of the Virgin Mary for God's people, an intercession rooted in her divine motherhood: we ask to "experience the intercession of her, through whom we were found worthy to receive the author of life, our Lord Jesus Christ, your Son" (Col);

—the example of the Mother of the Lord: like her the faithful are to "seek out and treasure the things that are [God's]" (PO).

Entrance Antiphon

In childbirth she brought forth the King, whose name is eternal.
She keeps a mother's joy with a virgin's honor.
None like her was seen before, and none thereafter.

COLLECT

O God, who through the fruitful virginity of Blessed Mary
bestowed on the human race the grace of eternal salvation,
grant, we pray,
that we may experience the intercession of her,
through whom we were found worthy to receive the author of life,
our Lord Jesus Christ, your Son.
Who lives and reigns with you in the unity of the Holy Spirit,
God, for ever and ever.

PRAYER OVER THE OFFERINGS

Accept, O Lord, the offerings we bring you
and grant that, enlightened by the Holy Spirit
and encouraged by the example of the Blessed Virgin Mary,
our hearts may always seek out and treasure the things that are yours.
Through Christ our Lord.

Preface P5, page 84.

Communion Antiphon John 1:14

The Word of God became flesh, and dwelt among us, full of grace and truth.

PRAYER AFTER COMMUNION

Renewed by the Body and Blood of your incarnate Word,
we pray, O Lord, that these divine mysteries,
which we have joyfully received
on this memorial of the Blessed Virgin Mary,
may make us sharers for eternity in the divinity of your Son.
Who lives and reigns for ever and ever.

6. THE BLESSED VIRGIN MARY AND THE EPIPHANY OF THE LORD

During Christmas Time the Church celebrates the mystery of the *revelation* or *manifestation* of the Word made flesh to all nations: first, to the Jews, represented by the humble shepherds, "the firstfruits of the Church from the people of Israel" (Pref), then to the Gentiles, represented by the wise men, "the firstfruits of the Church from the Gentiles" (Pref).

The following points seem especially noteworthy in this Mass:

—the celebration of *light*, signifying not only the glory of God the Father, which dawned upon Jerusalem (cf. 1 Read, Isaiah 60:1-6), bathing the shepherds in its glory (cf. Pref, cf. Luke 2:9), and in a marvelous way leading the wise men "by a shining star" (Pref, cf. Gos, Matthew 2:2, 9-10) to Christ; but also Jesus Christ, "the glory of Israel and the light of all nations" (Col, cf. Luke 2:32), whom the Father revealed to the world (cf. Col) and who in turn revealed to the world the glory of the Father (cf. PO);

—the celebration of *the role of Christ as Savior*. The many "christological titles" found in this formulary are of the greatest importance: Christ is the Son of God (cf. Col, PC) and Son of the Virgin (cf. PO, Pref); the "surpassing greatness of God" and "God's power," "the Most High," who "has chosen to be born as a little child" (Ent Ant); "the one Mediator and the Savior of the world" (Col), by whose birth we are saved (cf. PC), who gave "his whole life for our salvation" (PO). So the shepherds "acknowledged Christ as the Savior" when they saw the Son of the humble handmaid of the Lord (cf. Pref), and the wise men, when they found the child with his Mother, "worshiped him as God, proclaimed him as King, and acknowledged him as Redeemer" (Pref);

—the celebration of *the mystery of the Church*, which is foreshadowed in the holy city, Jerusalem (cf. 1 Read, Isaiah 60:1-6), and which seems to signify the house where the child is found with his Mother (cf. Gos, Matthew 2:11); the Church is founded on faith in Christ (cf. Col), and is gathered equally from Israel and the Gentiles (cf. Pref), since the Father draws "the families of all peoples to faith in the Gospel" (Pref);

—the celebration of *the ministry of the Virgin* in the Epiphany of the Lord, as several texts make clear: "The surpassing greatness of God has shone around us, God's power has been revealed through a virgin" (Ent Ant); "through the Blessed Virgin Mary you revealed your Son to the world" (Col); "through the ministry of the Blessed Virgin you draw the families of all peoples to faith in the Gospel" (Pref).

Entrance Antiphon

The surpassing greatness of God has shone around us,
God's power has been revealed through a virgin;
the Most High has chosen to be born as a little child,
to show forth majesty and splendor in lowliness of birth.

COLLECT

Lord our God, through the Blessed Virgin Mary
you revealed your Son to the world
as the glory of Israel
and the light of all nations;
grant that as we follow his teaching and example
we may strengthen our faith in Christ
and acknowledge him to be the one Mediator
and the Savior of the world.
Who lives and reigns with you in the unity of the Holy Spirit,
God, for ever and ever.

PRAYER OVER THE OFFERINGS

Lord God, through the power of the Holy Spirit
consecrate these gifts,
the offering of joyful hearts,
on this memorial of the Blessed Virgin Mary;
let them become the Body and Blood of Christ,
who was born of the Virgin Mother
to reveal your glory
and to give his whole life for our salvation.
Who lives and reigns for ever and ever.

Preface P6, page 85.

Communion Antiphon Cf. Matthew 2:2

We have seen his star in the East,
and have come with gifts to adore the Lord.

PRAYER AFTER COMMUNION

May the mysteries we have received,
O Lord our God,
always show forth your mercy in us,
that we, who celebrate with steadfast love
this memorial of the Mother of your Son,
may be saved by his birth.
Who lives and reigns for ever and ever.

7. THE BLESSED VIRGIN MARY AND THE PRESENTATION OF THE LORD

This Mass commemorates the role of our Lady in the mystery of the presentation of the Lord (cf. Luke 2:27-35). With due observance of the law, the opportune time for its celebration is on a Saturday or weekday around 2 February.

Our Lady, who is given the title of "virgin daughter of Zion" (Pref) in this mystery of salvation:

—in accordance with the Law of Moses (cf. Leviticus 12:1-8) submitted to the ritual of purification after childbirth, although as the "purest of virgins" from her "chaste womb" she had "brought forth in purity the Son of the eternal Father" (Ent Ant);

—faithfully carried out the law of the firstborn (cf. Exodus 13:1-2), redeeming with the offering of the poor (cf. Luke 2:24; PO) her Son, "the author of the New Law" (Col), "the Redeemer of us all" (PO), "the glory of" the "people Israel and the light of all nations" (Pref; cf. Luke 2:32), "the Lord, the Savior of the world" (Com Ant);

—as "the handmaid of [God's] plan of salvation" (Pref) saw in her Son "the spotless Lamb, to be sacrificed on the altar of the Cross for our salvation" (Pref) and offered him to the Father.

This Mass recalls the prophecy of Simeon, who foretold that the child would be a sign of contradiction and that a sword of sorrow would pierce his Mother's heart (cf. Luke 2:34-35); it celebrates the close association between our Lady and her Son in the work of salvation: "Son and Mother are united in the one undivided love, in the one shared suffering, in the single will to do what pleases you" (Pref).

In fulfilling these roles in the mystery of salvation, our Lady is the exemplar of the Church. So we ask the Father that the virgin Church, "like the Virgin Mary" (PC), the handmaid of the Lord (cf. Luke 1:38), may "keep its faith unspotted, grow in hope of heaven, and deepen its heartfelt love for you" (Col), "serve you with undivided heart" (PC), and, "with the lamp of faith burning brightly, go out with joy to meet the Bridegroom" (PC; cf. Matthew 25:1, 4).

Entrance Antiphon

Hail, purest of virgins, from your chaste womb
you brought forth in purity the Son of the eternal Father.

COLLECT

Lord, grant that the Church,
the chaste Bride of Christ,
may keep unbroken the New Covenant of love
and, like your humble handmaid,
who presented to you in the temple
the author of the New Law,
may the Church keep its faith unspotted,
grow in hope of heaven,
and deepen its heartfelt love for you.
Through our Lord Jesus Christ, your Son,
who lives and reigns with you in the unity of the Holy Spirit,
God, for ever and ever.

PRAYER OVER THE OFFERINGS

Lord, let our prayers and offerings be acceptable to you
as we present them with joy in our hearts
on this memorial of the Blessed Virgin Mary,
who made the offering of the poor to redeem her Son,
himself the Redeemer of us all.
Who lives and reigns for ever and ever.

Preface P 7, page 86.

Communion Antiphon

**The Virgin stands, presenting her Son, born before the daystar;
Simeon takes him in his arms and proclaims to all peoples
that this is the Lord, the Savior of the world.**

PRAYER AFTER COMMUNION

**Lord God,
grant that by the power of the Sacrament we have received
the virgin Church, like the Virgin Mary,
may serve you with undivided heart,
be attentive to the voice of the Spirit,
and, with the lamp of faith burning brightly,
go out with joy to meet the Bridegroom.
Who lives and reigns for ever and ever.**

8. OUR LADY OF NAZARETH

The hidden life of our Lord at Nazareth belongs to the mystery of salvation, and is an example of holiness: in the home at Nazareth our Savior, subject to Mary and Joseph (cf. Luke 2:51), spent the greater part of his life on earth. The Roman Liturgy commemorates this mystery of salvation especially on the Sunday within the octave of Christmas, when it celebrates the Feast of the Holy Family of Jesus, Mary, and Joseph. Many particular Churches and religious institutes also give liturgical honor to the Mother of God under the title of "Our Lady of Nazareth." This title celebrates in particular the role of our Lady at Nazareth in the service of her Son and his work of salvation.

This Mass, with its two series of readings, celebrates:

—*the mystery of the incarnation of the Word* (cf. Pref, Col) and his self-emptying: "when the fullness of time had come, God sent his Son, born of a woman, born under the law" (1 Read, Galatians 4:4-7; cf. Col); at Nazareth, as a real child, he "advanced in wisdom and age and favor" (Gos, A, Luke 2:41-52), and "was subject" to his parents (Com Ant, Luke 2:51);

—*the life shared by the Mother with her Son*: in the home at Nazareth, "as the first disciple of her Son," our Lady "receives the message of the Gospel, treasures it in her heart, and reflects on it in her mind" (Pref);

—*the virginal relationship between Mary and Joseph*, united "in an unbreakable bond of chaste love" (Pref), sharing a humble life of prayer, silence, and work (cf. Pref), and partners in joy (cf. Ent Ant), in sorrow (cf. Gos, B, Luke 2:41-52), and in the upbringing of Christ (cf. Com Ant, Luke 2:51);

—*the Kingdom of God*, which is already present and active in the Holy Family of Nazareth, and which is built up on earth "silently" (PC) and among the disciples, whose life is hidden in Christ (cf. Col, Colossians 3:3).

Entrance Antiphon Proverbs 23:24a, 25

**Great joy fills a father's heart when his son is righteous.
Let your father and mother be glad,
let the one who gave you birth rejoice.**

COLLECT

**All-holy Father, in the wonder of your wisdom and love
you decreed that your Son should be born of a woman,
and be subject to her guidance;
grant that we may enter more and more
into the mystery of your incarnate Word
and with him lead a hidden life on earth
until, escorted by his Virgin Mother,
we may joyously enter your home in heaven.
Through our Lord Jesus Christ, your Son,
who lives and reigns with you in the unity of the Holy Spirit,
God, for ever and ever.**

PRAYER OVER THE OFFERINGS

**We offer you, O Lord,
these offerings of conciliation and praise,
humbly asking that,
following the example of the Virgin of Nazareth
we may present our very selves
as a holy sacrifice pleasing to you.
Through Christ our Lord.**

Preface P 8, page 88.

Communion Antiphon Luke 2:51

**Jesus went down with them and came to Nazareth,
where he was subject to them.**

PRAYER AFTER COMMUNION

**All-holy Father,
look with kindness on those you have strengthened
with the Sacrament from heaven,
so that, through the example
of the Blessed Virgin Mary,
we may work silently
at building up your kingdom on earth
and so enjoy its fulfillment in heaven,
in the company of your Son.
Who lives and reigns for ever and ever.**

9. OUR LADY OF CANA

In the Gospel narrative (John 2:1-12) the "sign of Cana" belongs to the mystery of the manifestation of the Lord. The Roman Liturgy celebrates it accordingly every year on the Solemnity of the Epiphany of the Lord: "Three mysteries mark this holy day: today the star leads the magi to the infant Christ; today water is changed into wine for the wedding feast; today Christ wills to be baptized by John in the river Jordan to bring us salvation" (LH, 6 January, Ant for the Canticle of Mary, evening prayer II). Again, the Second Sunday in Ordinary Time, Year C, specifically celebrates this "beginning of signs." In this manifestation of the Lord our Lady played an active part, and so the liturgy remembers her along with her Son in the text: "Blessed are you, Virgin Mary: through you your Son gave the first of his signs; the Bridegroom prepared the new wine for his Bride; through you the disciples learned to believe in their Master" (Com Ant).

This Mass, therefore, celebrates together the Lord Jesus, the Church as it develops out of the sign of Cana, and the Blessed Virgin Mary.

First of all, it celebrates *Christ the Lord*, who manifested his glory in this marvelous sign and revealed himself: as the Messiah promised by God (cf. Pref), as the Master to whom the disciples give their obedience in faith (cf. Ent Ant, Gos, Com Ant), as the Lord, whose commands are carried out by the servants (cf. Pref), as the new Moses (cf. 1 Read, Exodus 19:3-8a) and the author of the new and everlasting Covenant, and as the Bridegroom who for the Church, his Bride, at an hour here foreshadowed will "shed his Blood on the Cross" (Pref), when blood and water, the symbols of redemption, will flow from his pierced side.

This Mass celebrates *the Church*, the community of disciples who faithfully follow Christ (cf. PC) and "do what he commands" (Col, Pref), provide for the needs of the community and in "unity of mind and heart" foreshadow the coming of the kingdom (cf. PC); it celebrates the beloved Bride, for whom the Bridegroom provides the wedding feast, his daily gift to his Bride (cf. Pref).

Finally, this Mass celebrates *the Mother of Jesus*, who in the Father's wisdom and love was chosen to "play her part in the mysteries of our salvation" (P). Our Lady, in the role she fulfilled in the mystery of salvation in the days of her life on earth on behalf of the bride and bridegroom and of the disciples, continues to play her part on behalf of the whole Church as she now reigns in glory in heaven. With loving care for the good of the human family she begs her Son to help us in our needs (cf. Pref); she tells us to do "what he commands in the Gospel he has given" (Col). What is more, we must hold, in the light of the liturgy, that the Mother of Jesus, who was present at the wedding feast of Cana, is present at the eucharistic wedding feast of the Church. So the community of the faithful celebrates the Eucharist each day in union above all with the glorious Virgin Mary.

Entrance Antiphon Cf. John 2:1, 11

**There was a wedding at Cana of Galilee,
and the Mother of Jesus was there:
Christ revealed his glory, and his disciples believed in him.**

COLLECT

**All-holy Father,
in your divine wisdom and love
you chose that the Blessed Virgin Mary
should play her part
in the mysteries of our salvation;
grant that by heeding the words of Christ's Mother
we may do what he commands
in the Gospel he has given.
Who lives and reigns with you in the unity of the Holy Spirit,
God, for ever and ever.**

PRAYER OVER THE OFFERINGS

**Lord,
with loving hearts we bring you these gifts;
change them into the Body and Blood
of Jesus Christ, your Son,
who at the request of his Mother
changed water into wine
and by this miraculous sign
foreshadowed the hour of his Death and Resurrection.
Through Christ our Lord.**

Preface P 9, page 90.

Communion Antiphon

Blessed are you, Virgin Mary:
through you your Son gave the first of his signs;
the Bridegroom prepared the new wine for his Bride;
through you the disciples learned to believe in their Master.

PRAYER AFTER COMMUNION

Filled, Lord God, with the sacrificial meal
of the Body and Blood of Christ,
we ask that, in imitation of the Blessed Virgin Mary,
we may follow Christ faithfully,
provide for the needs of the Church,
and together foreshadow the coming of your kingdom
by our unity of mind and heart.
Through Christ our Lord.

LENT

During Lent the faithful are properly prepared to celebrate Easter by hearing the word of God more fully, by spending time in prayer, by doing penance, by recalling their own Baptism, and by following Christ along the way of the Cross. On this "Lenten journey" the liturgy presents the Blessed Virgin to the faithful as the model of the disciple who faithfully listens to the word of God and follows the footsteps of Christ to Calvary, there to die with him (cf. 2 Timothy 2:11). At the end of Lent during the Sacred Paschal Triduum the Blessed Virgin is presented to the faithful as the new Eve or the "new woman" who stands by the tree of life (cf. John 19:25), as the companion of Christ the "new man," and as the spiritual mother into whose maternal care the Lord entrusts all his followers (cf. John 19:26).

MASS FORMULARIES

10. Holy Mary, Disciple of the Lord
11. The Blessed Virgin Mary at the Foot of the Cross, I
12. The Blessed Virgin Mary at the Foot of the Cross, II
13. The Commending of the Blessed Virgin Mary
14. The Blessed Virgin Mary, Mother of Reconciliation

10. HOLY MARY, DISCIPLE OF THE LORD

Lent is a "journey" for the faithful, during which they "more diligently listen to the word of God and devote themselves to prayer with greater earnestness" (SC, art. 109), and during which they are ready to bear the Cross with greater zeal, so that with minds and hearts renewed they may reach a more worthy celebration of the Easter festival. In this way they show themselves true disciples of Christ, hearing his words and seeking to make them their own (cf. Luke 8:15), following in his footsteps in self-denial (cf. Matthew 16:24), and striving to stand by his Cross in faithful witness (cf. John 19:26).

Hence, if during Lent for a reasonable cause Mass is celebrated in honor of the Blessed Virgin Mary, the present formulary is suitable. In it the Mother of the Lord is presented as one who shows us "the example of a disciple, who is faithful to the words of life" (Col). Our Lady is the one who by a unique gift of God was the Mother of Christ, and above all was his "first and most perfect . . . disciple" (MC, no. 35).

This Mass underlines the importance of "the word of God" or "the word of salvation" in the life of Christ's disciples (cf. Col, PC). It begs divine wisdom for them (cf. PO), extols the most holy Law of the Lord and the just judgments of the Lord (Resp, cf. Psalm 19:8-11), and sets before the eyes of the faithful our Lady keeping the words of the Lord in her heart (cf. Ent Ant, Gos, Luke 2:41-52), so that they may imitate her example (cf. PC).

Among the texts of the Mass pride of place must go to the Preface ("His Mother, the Virgin Mary in her glory, is rightly called blessed . . ."), for in it we hear the voice of Christ echoing the praise of the woman in the crowd ("Blessed is the womb that carried you and the breasts at which you nursed! ") in his reply: "Rather, blessed are those who hear the word of God and observe it!" (Luke 11:27-28). It recalls the explanation by St. Augustine of the Gospel passage "Who is my mother?" (Mark 3:33): "Holy Mary clearly carried out the will of the Father, and therefore it is a greater thing for her to be a disciple of Christ than to be his mother. She is more blessed in being a disciple of Christ than in being the mother of Christ" (*Sermo* 25, 7: PL 38, 937).

Entrance Antiphon

How favored are you, Mary!
You received the angel's message
and became the Mother of God's Word.
How favored are you, for you kept in your heart
those words from heaven and became the disciple of God's Word.

COLLECT

Lord our God, through the Blessed Virgin Mary
you have shown us the example of a disciple,
who is faithful to the words of life;
open our hearts to receive your saving word,
so that by the power of the Holy Spirit
it may speak to us in our daily lives
and bring forth a rich harvest of holiness.
Through our Lord Jesus Christ, your Son,
who lives and reigns with you in the unity of the Holy Spirit,
God, for ever and ever.

PRAYER OVER THE OFFERINGS

Lord God,
look with favor on the gifts
we offer with grateful hearts
on this memorial of the Blessed Virgin Mary,
mother and disciple of your Son;
grant that through these gifts we may receive
grace and wisdom in abundance,
for these are beyond our human strength.
Through Christ our Lord.

Preface P 10, page 91.

Communion Antiphon Luke 11:28

Blessed are they who hear the word of God and keep it!

PRAYER AFTER COMMUNION

**Lord God,
filled with the joy that comes from this Sacrament,
we ask that by imitating the Blessed Virgin Mary
we may be true disciples of Christ,
eagerly hearing his words
and putting them into practice.
Through Christ our Lord.**

11. THE BLESSED VIRGIN MARY AT THE FOOT OF THE CROSS

I

Lent unfolds like the journey of Jesus to the holy city of Jerusalem, the place of his sacrifice: as it progresses, there is more frequent meditation on the mystery of his Passion. So too in the hearts of the faithful there is more frequent remembrance of the compassion of our Lady.

In the propers of Masses of particular Churches and of religious institutes there are many formularies in honor of the Mother sharing in the Passion of her Son. The formulary set out here, with the exception of the Preface, comes from the *Proprium missarum Ordinis Fratrum Servorum beatae Mariae Virginis*, Curia Generalis OSM, Rome, 1972, pp. 24–27.

The texts of the Mass reflect on the mystery of Christ's Passion, mysteriously filled out through the present sufferings of his members as they face the "many trials of this life" (Col). The words of the Apostle: "in my flesh I am filling up what is lacking in the afflictions of Christ on behalf of his Body, which is the Church" (Com Ant, Colossians 1:24), are appropriately used in this celebration.

Our Lady, "queen of heaven and earth" (Gos Ver), stood by the Cross of her Son (cf. Ent Ant, Gos, John 19:25-27), "in his agony" (Col), "mournful" (Gos Ver), yet full of "courage" and "faith" (Pref), playing many roles in the mystery of salvation, and fulfilling "in her person the prophecies of old" (Pref). In relation to her Son, dying on the Cross, our Lady stands out as:

—*the handmaid of the Redeemer* (cf. PO), the Mother sharing his sufferings, united with the sacrifice of her Son, the High Priest (cf. PC);

—*the new Eve*, fulfilling the prophecy of the saving role of the "woman" (cf. Genesis 3:15; John 19:26; Revelation 12:1): as the first woman shared "in bringing death," so the second woman, Mary, shared "in restoring life" (Pref, cf. LG, no. 56);

—*the Mother of Zion*, acclaimed by all peoples as they say: "In you, all find their home" (Psalm 87:7), for she welcomes with a mother's love all who have been scattered but are now gathered into unity by "the Death of Christ" (Pref, John 11:52);

—*the image of the Church*, which as it looks on the Virgin "draws inspiration from her courage and keeps constant faith with its Bridegroom" (Pref, cf. LG, no. 64).

Entrance Antiphon John 19:25

There by the Cross of Jesus stood his Mother,
the sister of his Mother, Mary the wife of Cleophas,
and Mary Magdalene.

COLLECT

Lord our God,
in your mysterious wisdom
you fill out the Passion of Christ
through the suffering that his members endure
in the many trials of this life.
As you chose to have the mournful Mother
stand by your Son in his agony on the Cross,
grant that we too may bring love and comfort
to our brothers and sisters in distress.
Through our Lord Jesus Christ, your Son,
who lives and reigns with you in the unity of the Holy Spirit,
God, for ever and ever.

PRAYER OVER THE OFFERINGS

Lord,
graciously receive the offerings of your family
and make them the Sacrament of our redemption,
which Mary faithfully served
at the altar of the Cross.
Through Christ our Lord.

Preface P 11, page 92.

Communion Antiphon Colossians 1:24

In my flesh I am completing what is lacking in the afflictions of Christ on behalf of his Body, which is the Church.

PRAYER AFTER COMMUNION

Lord God, we have received the pledge of salvation
and now we offer this prayer.
Grant that the Holy Spirit, the Paraclete,
poured out upon your Church,
may descend in power on all peoples,
whom Christ, the High Priest,
claims as the reward of the sacrifice
he offered on the Cross
in the presence of his sorrowing Mother.
Through Christ our Lord.

12. THE BLESSED VIRGIN MARY AT THE FOOT OF THE CROSS

II

This Mass in celebration of Christ's saving Passion also honors the part played by the Blessed Virgin in achieving our salvation. When Mary became the Mother of Christ "by the power of the Holy Spirit" (Pref), she became by a further gift of divine love "a partner in his Passion" (Pref), a Mother suffering with him (Col, A, Col, B).

The beginning of the Mass echoes the prophecy of Simeon, which links the destiny of the Son and the Mother and foretells that Christ would be a sign that would be contested and that the Virgin's soul would be pierced by a sword of sorrow (cf. Ent Ant, Luke 2:34-35).

The prayers of the Mass recall the plan of salvation, by which God joined the suffering of the Mother with the suffering of her Son (Col, A, Col, B), and decreed that "the new Eve should stand by the Cross of the new Adam" (Pref).

The co-suffering of the Blessed Virgin in the drama of salvation is rightly celebrated, because she stood by the Cross of the Lord (cf. Gos, John 19:25-27) "firm in faith, strong in hope, burning with love" (Gos Ver); there she did not spare her own life when her nation was brought low (cf. 1 Read, Judith 13:17-20); she endured the greatest of pains in bringing forth to new and divine life the family of the Church, though she had brought forth her Son "without the pains of childbirth" (Pref); hence the faithful glorify her as they say, "How blessed was the Virgin Mary in her sufferings: she gained the palm of living martyrdom at the foot of the Cross of her Son" (Com Ant, A).

What took place in reality in the passion of Christ is now celebrated in sacramental signs; and so we pray that "the sacrifice of the altar, offered in union with the Virgin, may wipe away our sins and open for us the gates of heaven" (PO). The faithful, as they share in the sufferings of Christ, are to rejoice, "that [they] may also rejoice exultantly when his glory is revealed" (Com Ant, B, 1 Peter 4:13), and, by carrying their Cross each day, they may come to share in the resurrection of Christ (cf. PC).

The texts of the Mass come from the *Proprium missarum Ordinis Fratrum Servorum beatae Mariae Virginis*, Curia Generalis OSM, Rome, 1972, pp. 57–60.

Entrance Antiphon Luke 2:34-35

Simeon said to Mary: Behold, this child is destined
for the ruin and rising of many in Israel,
and to be a sign of contradiction;
and your own soul a sword will pierce.

COLLECT

A Lord our God,
you placed at the side of your suffering Son
his Mother to suffer with him,
so that the human race,
deceived by the wiles of the devil,
might become a new and resplendent creation.
Grant that your people may put aside their inheritance of sin
and put on the newness of life
won by Christ the Redeemer.
Who lives and reigns with you in the unity of the Holy Spirit,
God, for ever and ever.

B Lord God,
you decreed that the Mother of your Son
should stand by his Cross, suffering with him.
Safeguard in your family
the fruits of your great work of redemption
and in your goodness
make them grow daily more and more.
Through our Lord Jesus Christ, your Son,
who lives and reigns with you in the unity of the Holy Spirit,
God, for ever and ever.

PRAYER OVER THE OFFERINGS

Lord, let our gifts be consumed
by the fire of the Holy Spirit,
so that the sacrifice of the altar,
offered in union with the Virgin,
may wipe away our sins
and open for us the gates of heaven.
Through Christ our Lord.

Preface P 12, page 94.

Communion Antiphon

A How blessed was the Virgin Mary in her sufferings:
she gained the palm of living martyrdom at the foot of the Cross of her Son.

B Rejoice when you share in the sufferings of Christ, 1 Peter 4:13
that you may also rejoice exultantly when his glory is revealed.

PRAYER AFTER COMMUNION

**Lord God, protect your servants,
whose hunger and thirst
you have satisfied in this Sacrament;
as we call to mind Mary's suffering with Christ,
grant that by carrying our Cross each day
we may come to share in his Resurrection.
Who lives and reigns for ever and ever.**

13. THE COMMENDING OF THE BLESSED VIRGIN MARY

The words of Jesus, dying on the Cross: "Behold your son . . . Behold your mother" (John 19:26-27), are seen by the Church as a special parting gift, by which Christ the Lord "entrusted" to his Virgin Mother "all his disciples as her children" (Leo XIII, Encyclical Letter *Octobri mense:* ASS 24 [1891–1892] p. 195), and entrusted his Mother to his disciples to be honored and revered. Hence "a deep bond of love is fashioned between the Blessed Virgin Mary and his faithful disciples" (Pref), which is honored and celebrated in this Mass.

The commending of the disciples: it is primarily God who is glorified, for making "a home for the Blessed Virgin in the Church as the joyful mother of children" (Ent Ant, cf. Psalm 113:9). Our Lady is called "mother of those who believe" (Pref), to whom the faithful turn with full confidence; Jesus Christ is more than once referred to as the one who "entrusted us to his Virgin Mother as her children" (PC, cf. Col, PO, Pref). This act of commending is part of the mystery of Christ's Passion and the Virgin's co-suffering; the liturgy therefore refers to the Blessed Virgin as one who "stood by the Cross and tenderly looked on the wounds of her Son, whose Death she knew would redeem the world" (Gos Ver), and it places on her lips the words of the Apostle: "I endure all for the sake of the elect, so that they too may achieve salvation in Christ Jesus with eternal glory" (Com Ant, 2 Timothy 2:10). With Mary in mind the liturgy sets before the faithful the wonderful example of the mother of the Maccabees, who saw her sons dying, yet bore this with courage because of her hope in God (1 Read, 2 Maccabees 7:1, 20-29).

The commending of the Virgin: our Lady also was entrusted by Christ to the loving care of the beloved disciple: "To the virgin John, Christ, dying on the Cross, entrusted his Virgin Mother" (LH, 27 December, Ant 2 at morning prayer). In John Christ made all his disciples "living signs of his own love for her" (PO, cf. Ve 1276): they "receive her as a precious inheritance from their Master" (Pref), and in heeding what she says (cf. Pref, John 2:5) they conscientiously "keep the words of their Master" (Pref).

Entrance Antiphon Cf. Psalm 113:4, 9

The Lord is enthroned above all nations,
God's glory is above the heavens.
The Lord makes a home for the Blessed Virgin
in the Church as the joyful mother of children.

COLLECT

All-holy Father, you chose the Easter Mystery
as the way of our salvation;
grant that we, whom Jesus entrusted from the Cross
to his Virgin Mother,
may be numbered among your adopted children.
Through our Lord Jesus Christ, your Son,
who lives and reigns with you in the unity of the Holy Spirit,
God, for ever and ever.

PRAYER OVER THE OFFERINGS

Lord, receive the gifts we joyfully present,
that they may become the Body and Blood
of our Lord Jesus Christ,
who on the Cross entrusted all his followers
in the person of John
to the Virgin Mother as her children,
and entrusted her to them
as living signs of his own love for her.
He lives and reigns for ever and ever.

Preface P 13, page 95.

Communion Antiphon 2 Timothy 2:10

**I endure all for the sake of the elect,
so that they too may achieve salvation
in Christ Jesus with eternal glory.**

PRAYER AFTER COMMUNION

**Lord God,
let this sacred table increase our filial love,
for here we are nourished
by the Body and Blood of Christ,
who when dying on the Cross
delivered his spirit into your hands
and entrusted us to his Virgin Mother as her children.
Through Christ our Lord.**

14. THE BLESSED VIRGIN MARY, MOTHER OF RECONCILIATION

The season of Lent has both a baptismal and a penitential character (cf. SC, art. 109). From Ash Wednesday the words of the Apostle re-echo in the liturgy: "We implore you on behalf of Christ, be reconciled to God" (2 Corinthians 5:20). This text is also used in this Mass (1 Read, 2 Corinthians 5:17-21).

The Church has with ever greater clarity acknowledged the role of our Lady in reconciling sinners with God. The Fathers of the Church in the early centuries, in discussing the mystery of the Incarnation of the Word, speak frequently of the virginal womb of the Mother of the Lord as the place where "peace" between God and the human race came to be. The teaching of the Popes of our own age fits in admirably with this patristic thought: the Blessed Virgin, in the words of Pope John Paul II, "became associated with God in the very work of reconciliation through her divine maternity" (Postsynodal Apostolic Exhortation *Reconciliatio et paenitentiae*, no. 35: AAS 77 [1985], p. 275).

In the Middle Ages ecclesiastical writers, deepening their understanding of the maternal role of the Blessed Virgin, gave her the titles of "way of reconciliation," "general cause of reconciliation" as well as 'Mother of reconciliation," because it was from her that Jesus Christ, the "reconciliation of sinners," was born: "There is no reconciliation," says St. Anselm of Canterbury (d. 1109), "except the reconciliation that you bore in purity" (H. Barré, *Prières anciennes de l'Occident à la Mère du Sauveur*, Ed. P. Lethielleux, Paris, 1963, p. 305). Hence the faithful turn to the Blessed Virgin in order that, through her intercession, they may obtain "the grace of reconciliation," and, from the twelfth century at least, devoutly venerate her under the title of "refuge of sinners."

In our own day the Blessed Virgin is honored liturgically in many places under the title of "reconciler of sinners," thanks especially to the Missionaries of Our Lady of La Salette.

Hence, if Mass is celebrated during Lent in honor of our Lady, especially in sanctuaries where the faithful gather in large numbers for the Sacrament of Penance, this formulary is appropriate, extolling as it does the "mercies" of God "to all his creatures" (Ent Ant, A, Psalm 145:9) and honoring the Blessed Virgin for her "heart of compassion for sinners" (Pref).

Except for the Preface, almost all the Mass texts are taken from the *Missa propria beatae Mariae Virginis Reconciliatricis peccatorum*, Vatican Polyglot Press, 1978, pp. 4–6.

Entrance Antiphon

A The Lord is kind and full of compassion, Psalm 145:8-9
slow to anger,
abounding in mercy.
How good is the Lord to all,
compassionate to all his creatures.

B Hail, full of grace; you are called upon by sinners
because you are merciful
and look on our distress with compassion.

COLLECT

Lord our God, through the Precious Blood of your Son
you reconciled the world to yourself
and at the foot of his Cross
you chose the Blessed Virgin Mary
to be the Mother of reconciliation for sinners;
grant through her intercession
that we may obtain pardon for our sins.
Through our Lord Jesus Christ, your Son,
who lives and reigns with you in the unity of the Holy Spirit,
God, for ever and ever.

PRAYER OVER THE OFFERINGS

Lord, we offer you these gifts
of reconciliation and praise,
that through the intercession
of the Blessed Virgin Mary, refuge of sinners,
you may in your mercy pardon our sins
and steady our wavering hearts.
Through Christ our Lord.

Preface P 14, page 96.

Communion Antiphon

**Glorious things are spoken of you, O Mary,
for from you arose the sun of justice,
Christ our God.**

PRAYER AFTER COMMUNION

**Lord our God,
we have received the Body and Blood of your Son,
the Sacrament of our reconciliation;
grant through the intercession
of the Blessed Virgin Mary
that this Sacrament may bring us
the grace of your loving forgiveness
and the reward of eternal redemption.
Through Christ our Lord.**

EASTER TIME

During the "great Sunday," the fifty-day period in which with joyful exultation the Church celebrates the Paschal Mystery, the Roman Liturgy also commemorates the Mother of Christ as she was filled with joy because of the Resurrection of her Son and as she devoted herself to prayer with the Apostles in trusting expectation of the gift of the Holy Spirit (cf. Acts 1:14). When, in fulfillment of its maternal role, the Church celebrates the Sacraments of Christian Initiation—which are Paschal Sacraments—it acknowledges the Blessed Virgin as the model of this maternal role. The Church also accepts the Mother of Christ as its exemplar and helper in the mission of proclaiming the Gospel that Christ entrusted to it after his Resurrection from the dead (cf. Matthew 28:19-20).

MASS FORMULARIES

15. The Blessed Virgin Mary and the Resurrection of the Lord
16. Holy Mary, Fountain of Light and Life
17. Our Lady of the Cenacle
18. The Blessed Virgin Mary, Queen of Apostles

15. THE BLESSED VIRGIN MARY AND THE RESURRECTION OF THE LORD

In this Mass, the Collect and Communion Antiphon are taken from *The Roman Missal*, Common of the Blessed Virgin Mary, for Easter Time, the texts of which are notable for their teaching and beauty.

The Mass celebrates the Lord's Resurrection and the joy that flows from it:

—*to the whole world*, joy given by God the Father "by the Resurrection of your Son our Lord Jesus Christ" (Col); and so the day of the Lord's Resurrection was a "day of light and life when the night of death" was ended and "the whole world [was to] exult" (Pref).

—*to the infant Church*, which trembled "with joy at seeing again its immortal Lord" (Pref, cf. Luke 24:41; John 20:20).

—*to the Virgin Mother*, whose heart was filled "with joy beyond all telling" at the Resurrection of Christ (Pref).

The Church therefore greets the Virgin and invites her to rejoice: "Rejoice, O Virgin Mother, for Christ has risen from the tomb" (Com Ant); "Rejoice, Mother of Light: Jesus, the sun of justice, overcoming the darkness of the tomb, sheds his radiance over the whole world" (Ent Ant); "Hail, holy Mary, as you stood by the Cross in sorrow, you bore the sufferings of your Son, but now you are filled with serenity and joy" (*All*).

The Blessed Virgin, who conceived her Son in faith, and in faith looked forward to his Resurrection (cf. Pref), is the model of faith by which disciples acknowledge Christ, the child conceived by the Virgin Mary, to be truly God and truly human, and through the saving power of the Resurrection look forward to eternal happiness (cf. PC).

Entrance Antiphon

Rejoice, Mother of Light: Jesus, the sun of justice,
overcoming the darkness of the tomb,
sheds his radiance over the whole world, alleluia.

COLLECT

O God, who have been pleased to gladden the world
by the Resurrection of your Son our Lord Jesus Christ,
grant, we pray,
that through his Mother, the Virgin Mary,
we may receive the joys of everlasting life.
Through our Lord Jesus Christ, your Son,
who lives and reigns with you in the unity of the Holy Spirit,
God, for ever and ever.

PRAYER OVER THE OFFERINGS

As we observe this Memorial of the Blessed Virgin Mary,
we bring you our offerings, O Lord,
praying to be given strength by the humanity of Christ,
who offered himself to you on the Cross
as the unblemished oblation.
Who lives and reigns for ever and ever.

Preface P 15, page 97.

Communion Antiphon

Rejoice, O Virgin Mother,
for Christ has risen from the tomb, alleluia.

PRAYER AFTER COMMUNION

Confirm in our minds the mysteries of the true faith,
we pray, O Lord,
so that, confessing that he who was conceived of the Virgin Mary
is true God and true man,
we may, through the saving power of his Resurrection,
merit to attain eternal joy.
Through Christ our Lord.

16. HOLY MARY, FOUNTAIN OF LIGHT AND LIFE

The Sacraments of Christian Initiation, which are properly celebrated at the Easter Vigil, fashion the catechumens in the likeness of Christ: in the waters of Baptism they are made children of God, through the anointing and laying on of hands they are filled with the Holy Spirit, and through the heavenly bread and wine of the Eucharist they become one body with Christ.

The Fathers of the Church, however, frequently teach us that the mysteries of Christ, which the Church, our virgin mother, celebrates in the Sacraments of Christian Initiation, were "accomplished" in Mary, the Virgin Mother (Pref): the Spirit who sanctifies the womb of the Church—that is, the font of Baptism—to bring forth children of God, sanctified Mary's womb so that she might bring forth the firstborn of many brothers and sisters (cf. Hebrews 2:11-15); the same Spirit who, on the day of Pentecost, came down upon the Blessed Virgin with an abundance of gifts, comes down from heaven upon the newly baptized in the celebration of the Sacrament of Confirmation; the Body and Blood that Christ offered on the altar of the Cross for the life of the world and that the Church offers daily in the Eucharistic Sacrifice are the same Body and Blood that the Blessed Virgin Mary brought forth for our salvation.

This Mass commemorates the maternal role of both the Church and the Blessed Virgin in relation to the faithful. The motherhood of Mary is prior to the motherhood of the Church as type and model (cf. LG, no. 63).

The texts of the Mass celebrate our Lady as:

—*the Virgin Mother* (Col, cf. Pref) who, "overshadowed by the Holy Spirit" (Com Ant), became the Mother of Christ, the bread of life (cf. John 6:35), by whom the faithful are nourished in the Church.

—*the Mother of light* (Ent Ant), because she brought forth Christ, the light of the world (cf. John 12:46; Gos A, John 12:44-50).

—*the model of the Church* (Ent Ant), because the Church is itself a virgin and brings "to new birth in the chaste waters of Baptism a people of faith" (Ent Ant), and "in imitation of the Mother of Christ" makes its Eucharistic offering (PO); and because those things "accomplished in sign through the Sacraments of the Church" were "accomplished already in the Blessed Virgin" (Pref).

—*the sanctuary of the mysteries of God* (Com Ant), because she carried in her "virginal womb" Christ, the Sacrament of the Father: in Christ are hidden all the treasures of salvation and grace, and through him the face of the Father is revealed to us (cf. Luke 10:22; John 14:9).

This formulary, with its echoes of the Easter Vigil liturgy, is appropriately used on Saturdays of Easter Time when, for a reasonable cause and in accordance with liturgical law, Mass is celebrated in honor of the Blessed Virgin Mary.

Entrance Antiphon

Hail, Mother of light: a virgin, you gave birth to Christ,
and became the model of the Church, our mother,
bringing to new birth in the chaste waters of Baptism
a people of faith, alleluia.

COLLECT

Lord, from the chaste womb of the baptismal font
the Church, our mother, has given to children of this earth
a new birth as children of heaven.
Grant that through the life-giving Gospel
and your grace-filled Sacraments
the Church may form its daughters and sons
in the likeness of Christ, its founder,
who was born of a Virgin Mother
as the firstborn of many brothers and sisters
and the Savior of the whole human race.
Who lives and reigns with you in the unity of the Holy Spirit,
God, for ever and ever.

PRAYER OVER THE OFFERINGS

All-holy Father,
receive this offering
which the Church, our virginal mother,
makes in imitation of the Mother of Christ,
so that, gathered into unity
from every people and nation,
the Church may become one body,
living by the one Spirit.
Through Christ our Lord.

Preface P 16, page 98.

Communion Antiphon

Blessed are you, Virgin Mary:
you were overshadowed by the Holy Spirit
and bore in your virginal womb the Son of the eternal Father
and so became the sanctuary of the mysteries of God, alleluia.

PRAYER AFTER COMMUNION

Lord our God,
fill with the Spirit of Christ
those you have nourished with his Body,
so that our actions may always be guided
by that same Spirit,
who shines upon the pathways of the Church
and who sanctified the entire life of the Virgin Mother.
Through Christ our Lord.

17. OUR LADY OF THE CENACLE

Our Lady of the Cenacle is honored in the liturgy of several dioceses and religious families, especially in the Congregation of the Sisters of Our Lady of the Cenacle, founded by St. Therese Couderc (d. 1885).

The Church has come to see in our Lady, present at the first gathering of Christ's disciples (Ent Ant, cf. Acts 1:14), a mother cherishing the infant Church in her love and the supreme example of prayer in oneness of heart.

In this Mass formulary the Church gives glory to the Father in heaven for his gift of the Holy Spirit. Our Lady is here presented as:

—*the Virgin filled with the Holy Spirit:* God has poured out on her in abundance "the gifts of the Holy Spirit" (Col). The one "who was overshadowed by the Spirit at the Incarnation of the Word is once more filled with [this] Gift from on high at the birth of God's new people" (Pref);

—*model for the Church:* above all, she is the model of prayer, for God has given us a wonderful example of prayer in the Church at its beginning (cf. Pref), namely, the Mother of Jesus as she prays with the Apostles "in oneness of mind and heart" (Pref; cf. Ent Ant, Acts 1:14, cf. Col). The one "who waited in prayer for the coming of Christ is still at prayer as she calls upon the promised Paraclete" (Pref). A model, too, of harmony, unity, and peace (cf. Pref, PC); of obedience to the voice of the Holy Spirit (cf. PO); of watchfulness in waiting for the Second Coming of Christ (cf. Pref); of faithful observance of the word of God (cf. *All*, Luke 2:19) and eagerness to sow its seed.

Entrance Antiphon Cf. Acts 1:14

The disciples devoted themselves with one accord to prayer
with Mary, the Mother of Jesus, alleluia.

COLLECT

Lord our God,
as the Blessed Virgin was at prayer with the Apostles
you poured out on her in abundance
the gifts of the Holy Spirit;
grant through her intercession
that we too, being filled with the same Spirit,
may persevere with one mind in prayer
and bring to the world around us
the Good News of salvation.
Through our Lord Jesus Christ, your Son,
who lives and reigns with you in the unity of the Holy Spirit,
God, for ever and ever.

PRAYER OVER THE OFFERINGS

All-holy Father,
receive these gifts from joyful hearts
and grant that we may follow closely
the example of the Blessed Virgin Mary
by obeying the voice of the Spirit
and seeking to praise your glory in all things.
Through Christ our Lord.

Preface P 17, page 100.

Communion Antiphon Acts 2:42

The disciples continued steadfast in the teaching of the Apostles,
in communion of spirit, in the breaking of bread,
and in the practice of prayer, alleluia.

PRAYER AFTER COMMUNION

Lord God,
you have fed your holy people
with the one Bread of life;
renew us by the one gift of the Holy Spirit
and grant that under the protection of the Blessed Virgin
we may work for the unity and peace of all those
for whom your Son offered himself
as the sacrifice of our redemption.
Through Christ our Lord.

18. THE BLESSED VIRGIN MARY, QUEEN OF APOSTLES

Many religious institutes and societies of apostolic life have as their patroness the Blessed Virgin Mary at prayer in the Cenacle and honor her liturgically under the title of "Queen of Apostles." Prominent among these are the Society of the Catholic Apostolate, founded by Vincent Pallotti (d. 1850), the Pontifical Institute for Foreign Missions (P.I.M.E.), founded by Bishop Angelo Ramazzotti (d. 1861), the Pious Society of St. Paul for the Apostolate of the Press, and other institutes owing their origin to the Servant of God, Giacomo Alberione (d. 1971).

Many men and women in their apostolic and missionary zeal have noted the preeminent and "royal" position occupied by the Mother of Jesus in the community of the early Church and have recognized the importance of her presence at the events of Pentecost in relation to the spread of the Gospel message.

This Mass, except for the Preface, is taken from the *Proprium missarum Societatis Apostolatus Catholici*, Vatican Polyglot Press, 1972, pp. 3–6.

This formulary has great missionary value. The assembly of the faithful prays that the Church may spread, "by word and example, the glory of [God's] name" (Col), may "grow in number" (PO), and "may advance in the way of salvation" (PC).

The Preface celebrates God's "plan of salvation," in which the Blessed Virgin, guided by the Holy Spirit, hastened with the message of salvation to the house of Elizabeth, and "Peter and the other apostles," strengthened by the descent of the Spirit, moved out boldly from the Cenacle to preach the Gospel of Christ to all nations.

Entrance Antiphon Cf. Acts 1:14

The disciples devoted themselves with one accord to prayer
with Mary, the Mother of Jesus, alleluia.

COLLECT

O God, who gave the Holy Spirit to your Apostles
as they joined in prayer with Mary, the Mother of Jesus,
grant through her intercession
we may faithfully serve your majesty
and extend, by word and example, the glory of your name.
Through our Lord Jesus Christ, your Son,
who lives and reigns with you in the unity of the Holy Spirit,
God, for ever and ever.

PRAYER OVER THE OFFERINGS

By your favor, O Lord,
and through the intercession of Blessed Mary ever-Virgin,
may our offering obtain for your Church this grace,
that she may grow in the number of the faithful
and be ever radiant with an abundance of virtues
Through Christ our Lord.

Preface P 18, page 102.

Communion Antiphon Cf. Luke 11:27-28

Blessed is the womb that bore Christ the Lord;
blessed, rather, are those who hear the word of God and keep it.

PRAYER AFTER COMMUNION

Having partaken, O Lord, of these helps to our salvation
in our commemoration of the Blessed Virgin Mary,
Queen of Apostles,
we humbly beseech you,
that, persevering in your will
and in service of the human family,
your people may draw ever closer to salvation.
Through Christ our Lord.

THE ORDER OF MASS

THE INTRODUCTORY RITES

1. When the people are gathered, the Priest approaches the altar with the ministers while the Entrance Chant is sung.

When he has arrived at the altar, after making a profound bow with the ministers, the Priest venerates the altar with a kiss and, if appropriate, incenses the Cross and the altar. Then, with the ministers, he goes to the chair.

When the Entrance Chant is concluded, the Priest and the faithful, standing, sign themselves with the Sign of the Cross, while the Priest, facing the people, says:

In the name of the Father, and of the Son, and of the Holy Spirit.

The people reply:

Amen.

2. Then the Priest, extending his hands, greets the people, saying:

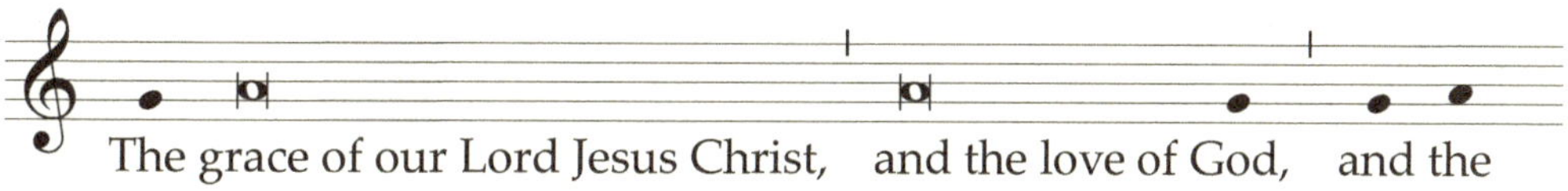

The grace of our Lord Jesus Christ,
and the love of God,
and the communion of the Holy Spirit
be with you all.

Or:

**Grace to you and peace from God our Father
and the Lord Jesus Christ.**

Or:

The Lord be with you.

The people reply:

And with your spirit.

In this first greeting a Bishop, instead of The Lord be with you, says:

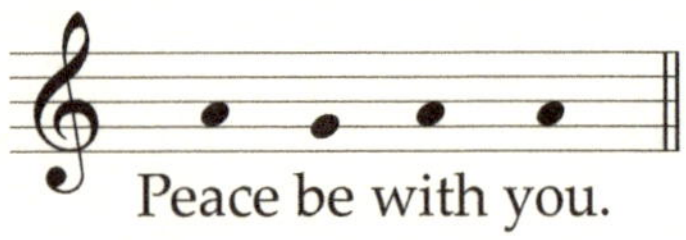

Peace be with you.

---

3. The Priest, or a Deacon, or another minister, may very briefly introduce the faithful to the Mass of the day.

Penitential Act

4. Then follows the Penitential Act, to which the Priest invites the faithful, saying:

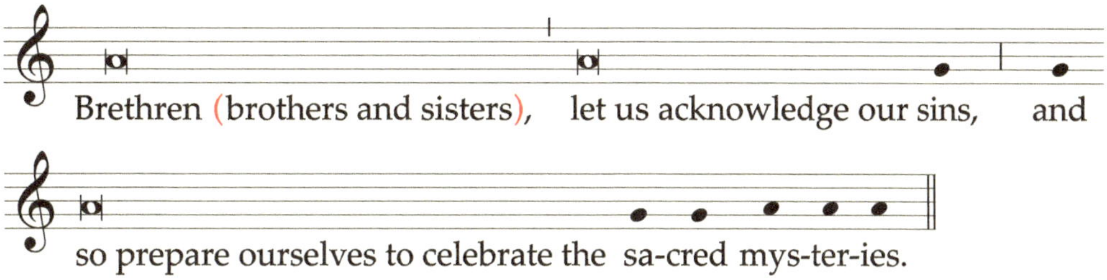

Brethren (brothers and sisters), let us acknowledge our sins,
and so prepare ourselves to celebrate the sacred mysteries.

A brief pause for silence follows. Then all recite together the formula of general confession:

I confess to almighty God
and to you, my brothers and sisters,
that I have greatly sinned,
in my thoughts and in my words,
in what I have done and in what I have failed to do,

And, striking their breast, they say:

through my fault, through my fault,
through my most grievous fault;

Then they continue:

therefore I ask blessed Mary ever-Virgin,
all the Angels and Saints,
and you, my brothers and sisters,
to pray for me to the Lord our God.

The absolution by the Priest follows:

May almighty God have mercy on us,
forgive us our sins,
and bring us to everlasting life.

The people reply:

Amen.

Or:

5. The Priest invites the faithful to make the Penitential Act:

Brethren (brothers and sisters), let us acknowledge our sins, and so prepare ourselves to celebrate the sacred mysteries.

A brief pause for silence follows.

The Priest then says:

Have mercy on us, O Lord.

The people reply:

For we have sinned against you.

The Priest:

Show us, O Lord, your mercy.

The people:

And grant us your salvation.

The absolution by the Priest follows:

May almighty God have mercy on us,
forgive us our sins,
and bring us to everlasting life.

The people reply:

Amen.

Or:

6. The Priest invites the faithful to make the Penitential Act:

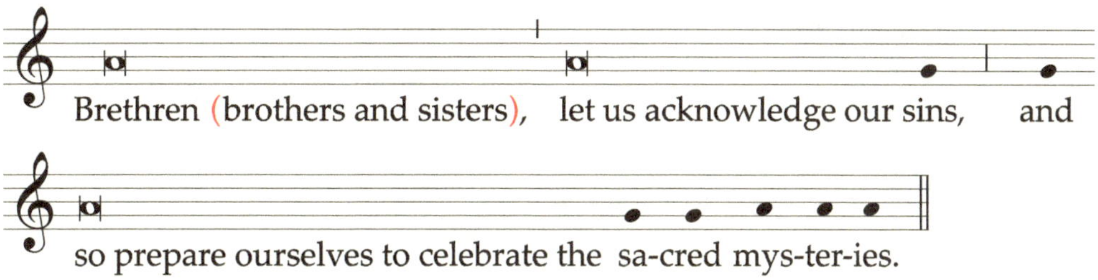

Brethren (brothers and sisters), let us acknowledge our sins,
and so prepare ourselves to celebrate the sacred mysteries.

A brief pause for silence follows.

The Priest, or a Deacon or another minister, then says the following or other invocations with Kyrie, eleison (Lord, have mercy):

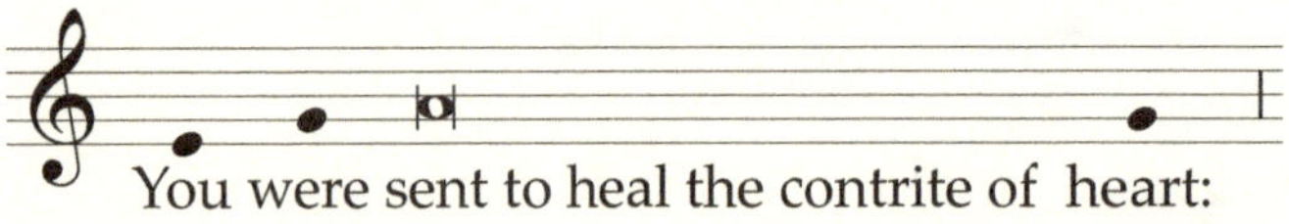

You were sent to heal the contrite of heart:

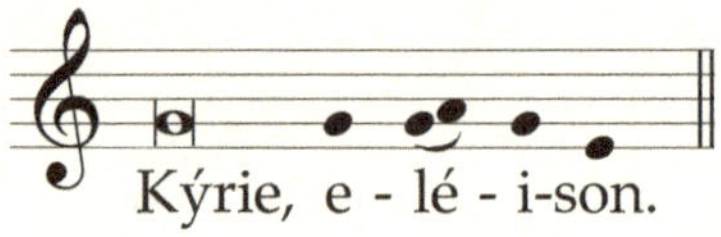

Lord, have mercy. Or: **Kyrie, eleison.**

The people reply:

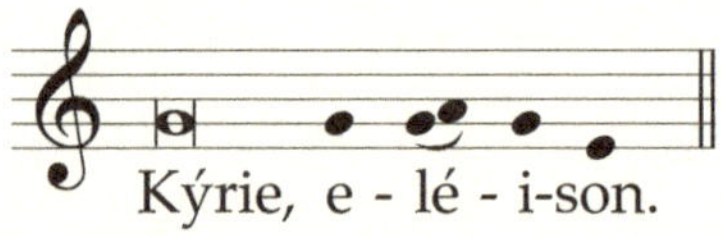

Lord, have mercy. Or: Kyrie, eleison.

The Priest:

You came to call sinners:

Christ, have mercy. Or: **Christe, eleison.**

The people:

Christ, have mercy. Or: Christe, eleison.

The Priest:

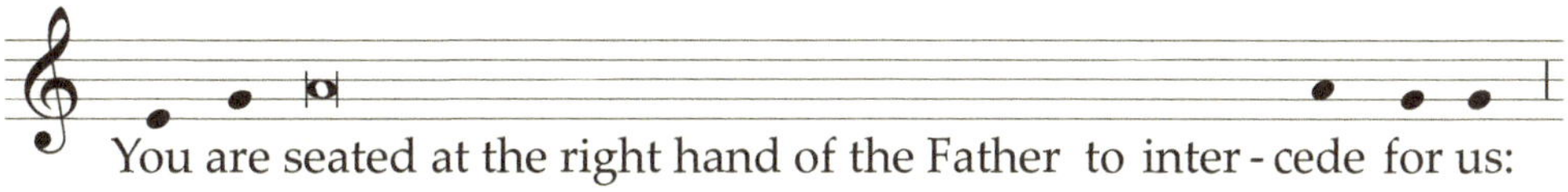

You are seated at the right hand of the Father to intercede for us:

Lord, have mercy. Or: **Kyrie, eleison.**

The people:

Lord, have mercy. Or: Kyrie, eleison.

The absolution by the Priest follows:

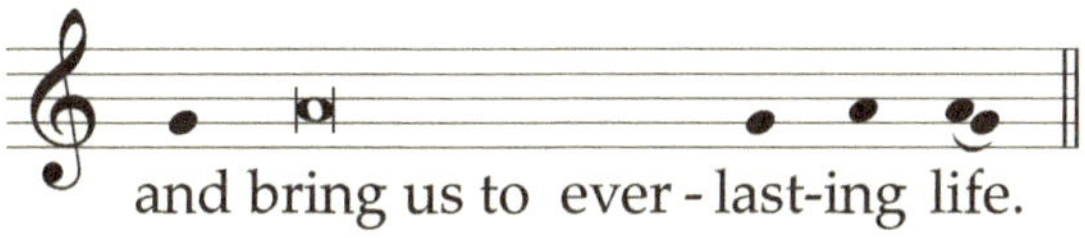

May almighty God have mercy on us,
forgive us our sins,
and bring us to everlasting life.

The people reply:

Amen.

7. The Kyrie, eleison (Lord, have mercy) invocations follow, unless they have just occurred in a formula of the Penitential Act.

℣. Lord, have mercy. **℟. Lord, have mercy.**
℣. Christ, have mercy. **℟. Christ, have mercy.**
℣. Lord, have mercy. **℟. Lord, have mercy.**

Or:

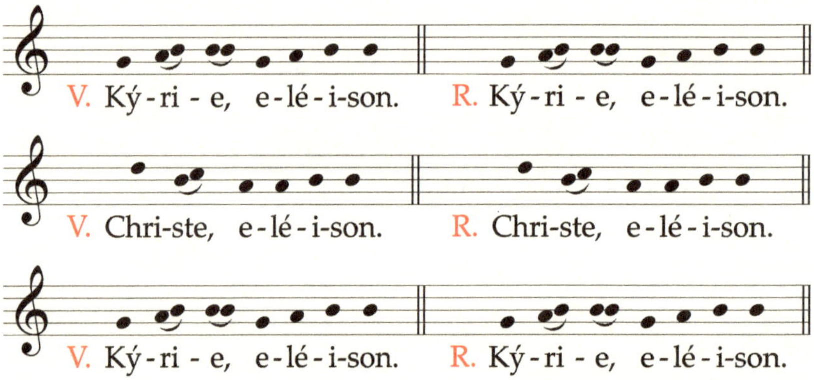

Or:

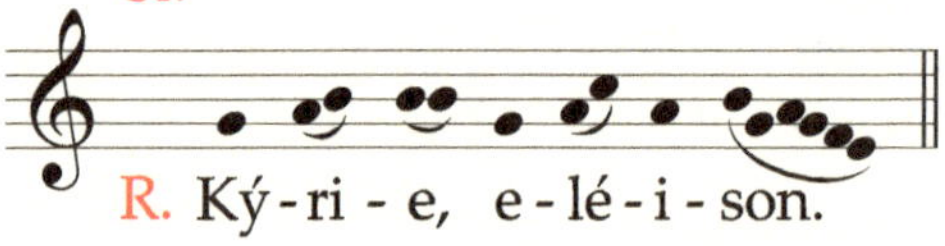

℣. Kyrie, eleison. **℟. Kyrie, eleison.**
℣. Christe, eleison. **℟. Christe, eleison.**
℣. Kyrie, eleison. **℟. Kyrie, eleison.**

8. Then, when it is prescribed, this hymn is either sung or said:

Glory to God in the highest,
and on earth peace to people of good will.

We praise you,
we bless you,
we adore you,
we glorify you,
we give you thanks for your great glory,
Lord God, heavenly King,
O God, almighty Father.

Lord Jesus Christ, Only Begotten Son,
Lord God, Lamb of God, Son of the Father,
you take away the sins of the world,
have mercy on us;
you take away the sins of the world,
receive our prayer;
you are seated at the right hand of the Father,
have mercy on us.

For you alone are the Holy One,
you alone are the Lord,
you alone are the Most High,
Jesus Christ,
with the Holy Spirit,
in the glory of God the Father.
Amen.

9. When this hymn is concluded, the Priest, with hands joined, says:

Let us pray.

And all pray in silence with the Priest for a while.

Then the Priest, with hands extended, says the Collect prayer, at the end of which the people acclaim:

Amen.

THE LITURGY OF THE WORD

10. Then the reader goes to the ambo and reads the First Reading, while all sit and listen.

To indicate the end of the reading, the reader acclaims:

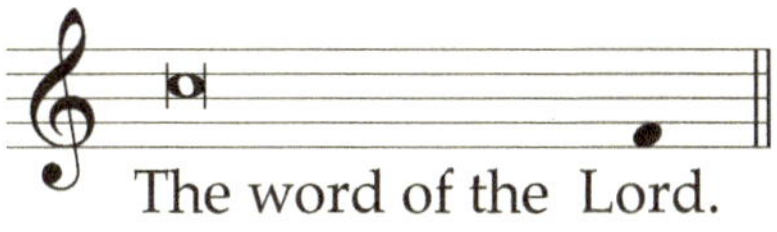

The word of the Lord.

All reply:

Thanks be to God.

11. The psalmist or cantor sings or says the Psalm, with the people making the response.

12. After this, if there is to be a Second Reading, a reader reads it from the ambo, as above.

To indicate the end of the reading, the reader acclaims:

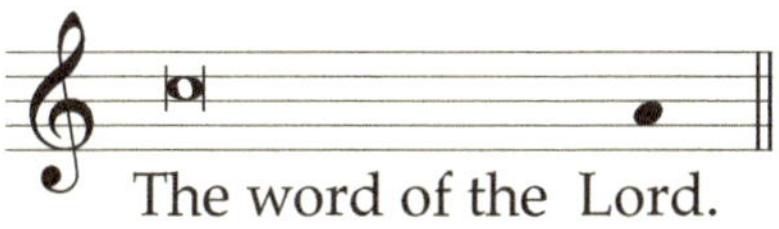

The word of the Lord.

All reply:

Thanks be to God.

13. There follows the Alleluia or another chant laid down by the rubrics, as the liturgical time requires.

14. Meanwhile, if incense is used, the Priest puts some into the thurible. After this, the Deacon who is to proclaim the Gospel, bowing profoundly before the Priest, asks for the blessing, saying in a low voice:

Your blessing, Father.

The Priest says in a low voice:

May the Lord be in your heart and on your lips,
that you may proclaim his Gospel worthily and well,
in the name of the Father, and of the Son, ✠ and of the Holy Spirit.

The Deacon signs himself with the Sign of the Cross and replies:

Amen.

If, however, a Deacon is not present, the Priest, bowing before the altar, says quietly:

Cleanse my heart and my lips, almighty God,
that I may worthily proclaim your holy Gospel.

15. The Deacon, or the Priest, then proceeds to the ambo, accompanied, if appropriate, by ministers with incense and candles. There he says:

The Lord be with you.

The people reply:

And with your spirit.

The Deacon, or the Priest:

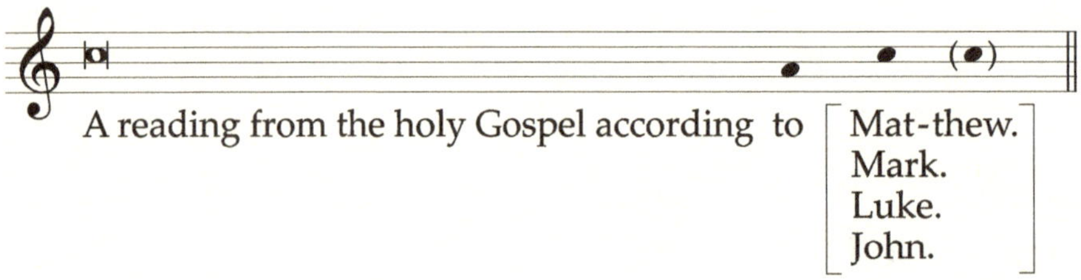

A reading from the holy Gospel according to N.

and, at the same time, he makes the Sign of the Cross on the book and on his forehead, lips, and breast.

The people acclaim:

Glory to you, O Lord.

Then the Deacon, or the Priest, incenses the book, if incense is used, and proclaims the Gospel.

16. At the end of the Gospel, the Deacon, or the Priest, acclaims:

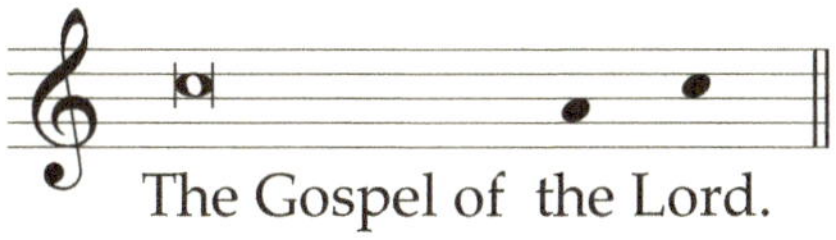

The Gospel of the Lord.

All reply:

Praise to you, Lord Jesus Christ.

Then he kisses the book, saying quietly:

Through the words of the Gospel
may our sins be wiped away.

17. Then follows the Homily, which is to be preached by a Priest or Deacon on all Sundays and Holydays of Obligation; on other days, it is recommended.

18. At the end of the Homily, the Symbol or Profession of Faith or Creed, when prescribed, is either sung or said:

Light from Light, true God from true God, be-got-ten, not made,
con-sub-stan-tial with the Fa-ther; through him all things were
made. For us men and for our sal-va-tion he came down from
At the words that follow, up to and including and became man, all bow.
heav-en, and by the Ho-ly Spir-it was in-car-nate of the Vir-gin
Mar-y, and be-came man.
For our sake he was cru-ci-fied un-der Pon-tius Pi-late, he
suffered death and was bur-ied, and rose a-gain on the third day
in accordance with the Scrip-tures. He as-cend-ed in-to heav-en
and is seated at the right hand of the Fa-ther. He will come a-gain
in glo-ry to judge the living and the dead and his kingdom will
have no end.
I be-lieve in the Ho-ly Spir-it, the Lord, the giv-er of life, who
pro-ceeds from the Father and the Son, who with the Fa-ther and

**I believe in one God,
the Father almighty,
maker of heaven and earth,
of all things visible and invisible.**

**I believe in one Lord Jesus Christ,
the Only Begotten Son of God,
born of the Father before all ages.
God from God, Light from Light,
true God from true God,
begotten, not made, consubstantial with the Father;
through him all things were made.
For us men and for our salvation
he came down from heaven,**

At the words that follow, up to and including and became man, all bow.

**and by the Holy Spirit was incarnate of the Virgin Mary,
and became man.**

**For our sake he was crucified under Pontius Pilate,
he suffered death and was buried,
and rose again on the third day
in accordance with the Scriptures.**

He ascended into heaven
and is seated at the right hand of the Father.
He will come again in glory
to judge the living and the dead
and his kingdom will have no end.

I believe in the Holy Spirit, the Lord, the giver of life,
who proceeds from the Father and the Son,
who with the Father and the Son is adored and glorified,
who has spoken through the prophets.

I believe in one, holy, catholic and apostolic Church.
I confess one Baptism for the forgiveness of sins
and I look forward to the resurrection of the dead
and the life of the world to come. Amen.

19. Instead of the Niceno-Constantinopolitan Creed, especially during Lent and Easter Time, the baptismal Symbol of the Roman Church, known as the Apostles' Creed, may be used.

I believe in God,
the Father almighty,
Creator of heaven and earth,
and in Jesus Christ, his only Son, our Lord,

At the words that follow, up to and including the Virgin Mary, all bow.

who was conceived by the Holy Spirit,
born of the Virgin Mary,
suffered under Pontius Pilate,
was crucified, died and was buried;
he descended into hell;
on the third day he rose again from the dead;
he ascended into heaven,
and is seated at the right hand of God the Father almighty;
from there he will come to judge the living and the dead.

I believe in the Holy Spirit,
the holy catholic Church,
the communion of saints,
the forgiveness of sins,
the resurrection of the body,
and life everlasting. Amen.

20. Then follows the Universal Prayer, that is, the Prayer of the Faithful or Bidding Prayers.

The Liturgy of the Eucharist

21. When all this has been done, the Offertory Chant begins. Meanwhile, the ministers place the corporal, the purificator, the chalice, the pall, and the Missal on the altar.

22. It is desirable that the faithful express their participation by making an offering, bringing forward bread and wine for the celebration of the Eucharist and perhaps other gifts to relieve the needs of the Church and of the poor.

23. The Priest, standing at the altar, takes the paten with the bread and holds it slightly raised above the altar with both hands, saying in a low voice:

Blessed are you, Lord God of all creation,
for through your goodness we have received
the bread we offer you:
fruit of the earth and work of human hands,
it will become for us the bread of life.

Then he places the paten with the bread on the corporal.

If, however, the Offertory Chant is not sung, the Priest may speak these words aloud; at the end, the people may acclaim:

Blessed be God for ever.

24. The Deacon, or the Priest, pours wine and a little water into the chalice, saying quietly:

By the mystery of this water and wine
may we come to share in the divinity of Christ
who humbled himself to share in our humanity.

25. The Priest then takes the chalice and holds it slightly raised above the altar with both hands, saying in a low voice:

Blessed are you, Lord God of all creation,
for through your goodness we have received
the wine we offer you:
fruit of the vine and work of human hands,
it will become our spiritual drink.

Then he places the chalice on the corporal.

If, however, the Offertory Chant is not sung, the Priest may speak these words aloud; at the end, the people may acclaim:

Blessed be God for ever.

26. After this, the Priest, bowing profoundly, says quietly:

With humble spirit and contrite heart
may we be accepted by you, O Lord,

and may our sacrifice in your sight this day
be pleasing to you, Lord God.

27. If appropriate, he also incenses the offerings, the Cross, and the altar. A Deacon or other minister then incenses the Priest and the people.

28. Then the Priest, standing at the side of the altar, washes his hands, saying quietly:

Wash me, O Lord, from my iniquity
and cleanse me from my sin.

29. Standing at the middle of the altar, facing the people, extending and then joining his hands, he says:

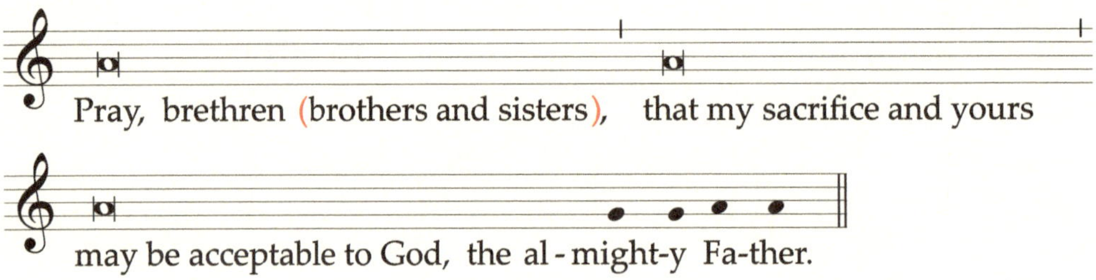

Pray, brethren (brothers and sisters),
that my sacrifice and yours
may be acceptable to God,
the almighty Father.

The people rise and reply:

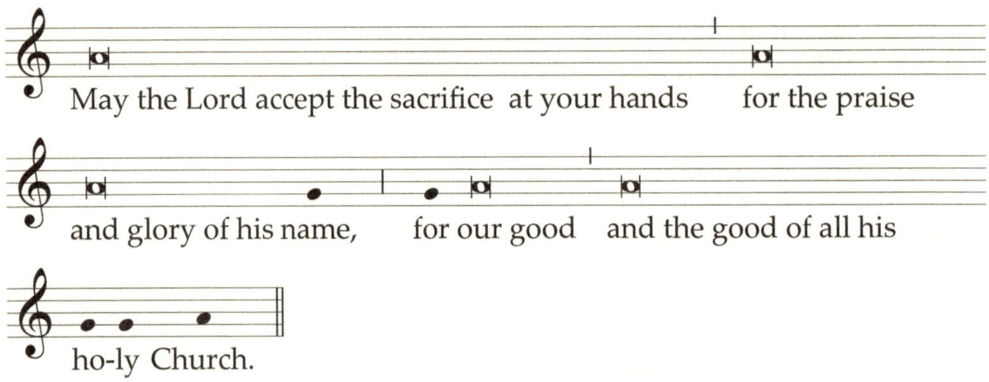

May the Lord accept the sacrifice at your hands
for the praise and glory of his name,
for our good
and the good of all his holy Church.

30. Then the Priest, with hands extended, says the Prayer over the Offerings, at the end of which the people acclaim:

Amen.

THE EUCHARISTIC PRAYER

31. Then the Priest begins the Eucharistic Prayer.

Extending his hands, he says:

The Lord be with you.

The people reply:

And with your spirit.

The Priest, raising his hands, continues:

Lift up your hearts.

The people:

We lift them up to the Lord.

The Priest, with hands extended, adds:

Let us give thanks to the Lord our God.

The people:

It is right and just.

The Priest, with hands extended, continues the Preface.

At the end of the Preface he joins his hands and concludes the Preface with the people, singing or saying aloud:

Holy, Holy, Holy Lord God of hosts.
Heaven and earth are full of your glory.
Hosanna in the highest.
Blessed is he who comes in the name of the Lord.
Hosanna in the highest.

Or:

32. In Eucharistic Prayer I, the Roman Canon, the words included in brackets may be omitted.

MARY, CHOSEN DAUGHTER OF ISRAEL P 1

Our Lady Is Daughter Of Adam, Child Of Abraham, Branch Of Jesse

Priest: **The Lord be with you.**
People: **And with your spirit.**

Priest: **Lift up your hearts.**
People: **We lift them up to the Lord.**

Priest: **Let us give thanks to the Lord our God.**
People: **It is right and just.**

**It is truly right and just, our duty and our salvation,
always and everywhere to give you thanks,
Lord, holy Father, almighty and eternal God.**

**For you chose the Blessed Virgin Mary
as the crown of Israel and the beginning of the Church,
to reveal to all peoples that salvation is born from Israel
and that your new family springs from a chosen root.**

**She is by nature the daughter of Adam,
who by her sinlessness undid the sin of Eve.
She is by faith the true child of Abraham,
who first believed and so conceived.
She is by descent the branch from the root of Jesse,
bearing the flower that is Jesus Christ our Lord.**

**Through him the Angels of heaven
offer their prayer of adoration
as they rejoice in your presence for ever.
May our voices be one with theirs
in their triumphant hymn of praise:**

Holy, Holy, Holy Lord God of hosts . . .

MARY AND THE ANNUNCIATION OF THE LORD P 2

The Blessed Virgin Received The Angel's Message In Faith

Priest: **The Lord be with you.**
People: **And with your spirit.**

Priest: **Lift up your hearts.**
People: **We lift them up to the Lord.**

Priest: **Let us give thanks to the Lord our God.**
People: **It is right and just.**

**It is truly right and just, our duty and our salvation,
always and everywhere to give you thanks,
Lord, holy Father, almighty and eternal God,
through Christ our Lord.**

**For the Virgin Mary heard with faith
that the Christ was to be born among men and for men's sake
by the overshadowing power of the Holy spirit.
Lovingly she bore him in her immaculate womb,
that the promises to the children of Israel might come about
and the hope of nations be accomplished beyond all telling.**

**Through him the host of Angels adores your majesty
and rejoices in your presence for ever.
May our voices, we pray, join with theirs
in one chorus of exultant praise, as we acclaim:**

Holy, Holy, Holy Lord God of hosts . . .

THE VISITATION OF THE BLESSED VIRGIN MARY P 3

Holy Mary, Blessed for Her Belief in the Promise of Salvation

Priest: **The Lord be with you.**
People: **And with your spirit.**

Priest: **Lift up your hearts.**
People: **We lift them up to the Lord.**

Priest: **Let us give thanks to the Lord our God.**
People: **It is right and just.**

**It is truly right and just, our duty and our salvation,
always and everywhere to give you thanks,
Lord, holy Father, almighty and eternal God,
through Christ our Lord.**

**For by your Holy Spirit
you inspired Elizabeth
to reveal the surpassing honor
you have given to the Blessed Virgin Mary.**

**Mary is rightly hailed as blessed
because she believed in your promise of salvation;
in her act of loving service
she is greeted as Mother of the Lord
by the Mother of Christ's herald.**

**We make our own the canticle of joy
on the lips of God's Virgin Mother,
and in our lowliness we too proclaim your greatness
in the never-ending hymn
of the whole company of Angels and Saints
as they cry out:**

Holy, Holy, Holy Lord God of hosts . . .

MARY, MOTHER OF GOD P 4

Holy Mary Rejoiced Because as a Virgin She Gave Birth to the Redeemer

Priest: **The Lord be with you.**
People: **And with your spirit.**

Priest: **Lift up your hearts.**
People: **We lift them up to the Lord.**

Priest: **Let us give thanks to the Lord our God.**
People: **It is right and just.**

**It is truly right and just, our duty and our salvation,
always and everywhere to give you thanks,
Lord, holy Father, almighty and eternal God.**

**For by a wonderful and inexpressible mystery
the Blessed Virgin conceived your only Son
and bore in her pure womb the Lord of heaven.**

**She who knew not man becomes a mother;
she who has given birth remains a virgin.
What joy is hers at your twofold gift:
she is full of wonder at her virgin-motherhood
and full of joy at giving birth to the Redeemer.**

**Through him the Angels of heaven
offer their prayer of adoration
as they rejoice in your presence for ever.
May our voices be one with theirs
in their triumphant hymn of praise:**

Holy, Holy, Holy Lord God of hosts . . .

MARY, MOTHER OF THE SAVIOR P 5

The Savior Comes Forth from Mary as the Bridegroom of the Church

Priest: **The Lord be with you.**
People: **And with your spirit.**

Priest: **Lift up your hearts.**
People: **We lift them up to the Lord.**

Priest: **Let us give thanks to the Lord our God.**
People: **It is right and just.**

**It is truly right and just, our duty and our salvation,
always and everywhere to give you thanks,
Lord, holy Father, almighty and eternal God,
especially as we celebrate this holy season (of Christmas).**

**When Mary brought forth her child
from the secret shrine of her virginal womb
you revealed as a light for all nations
the sign and source of our salvation,
your Son, Jesus Christ.**

**Like the rising sun,
the Bridegroom of the Church
has dawned upon us to rescue us
from darkness and the shadow of death
and to make us a kingdom of unfailing light.**

**In our joy we sing to your glory
with all the choirs of Angels:**

Holy, Holy, Holy Lord God of hosts . . .

MARY AND THE EPIPHANY OF THE LORD P 6

Christ Is Revealed to the World Through the Ministry of the Virgin

Priest: **The Lord be with you.**
People: **And with your spirit.**

Priest: **Lift up your hearts.**
People: **We lift them up to the Lord.**

Priest: **Let us give thanks to the Lord our God.**
People: **It is right and just.**

**It is truly right and just, our duty and our salvation,
always and everywhere to give you thanks,
Lord, holy Father, almighty and eternal God.**

**For through the ministry of the Blessed Virgin
you draw the families of all peoples
to faith in the Gospel.**

**The shepherds, bathed in your glory
and enlightened by choirs of Angels,
acknowledged Christ as the Savior
and became the firstfruits of the Church
from the people of Israel.**

**The wise men, inspired by grace
and led by a shining star,
entered a lowly house,
found the child with his Mother,
and, as the firstfruits of the Church from the Gentiles,
worshiped him as God,
proclaimed him as King,
and acknowledged him as Redeemer.**

**Through him the Angels of heaven
offer their prayer of adoration
as they rejoice in your presence for ever.
May our voices be one with theirs
in their triumphant hymn of praise:**

Holy, Holy, Holy Lord God of hosts . . .

MARY AND THE PRESENTATION OF THE LORD P 7

Our Lady Is the Handmaid of God's Plan of Salvation

Priest: **The Lord be with you.**
People: **And with your spirit.**

Priest: **Lift up your hearts.**
People: **We lift them up to the Lord.**

Priest: **Let us give thanks to the Lord our God.**
People: **It is right and just.**

**It is truly right to give you thanks,
truly just to give you glory, Father most holy,
as we celebrate this memorial of the Blessed Virgin Mary.**

**She is the virgin daughter of Zion
who, in fulfillment of the Law,
presents to you her Son,
the glory of your people Israel
and the light of all nations.**

**She is the Virgin,
the handmaid of your plan of salvation,
who presents to you the spotless Lamb,
to be sacrificed on the altar of the Cross
for our salvation.**

**She is the Virgin Mother
who rejoices in this child of blessing,
is saddened by the prophecy of Simeon,
but who exults that your people
go out to meet their Savior.**

Lord, we see your providence
as Son and Mother are united
in the one undivided love,
in the one shared suffering,
in the single will to do what pleases you.

In our joy we sing to your glory
with all the choirs of Angels:

Holy, Holy, Holy Lord God of hosts . . .

OUR LADY OF NAZARETH P 8

The Daily Life of Our Lady in the Home at Nazareth

Priest: **The Lord be with you.**
People: **And with your spirit.**

Priest: **Lift up your hearts.**
People: **We lift them up to the Lord.**

Priest: **Let us give thanks to the Lord our God.**
People: **It is right and just.**

It is truly right to give you thanks,
truly just to give you glory, Father most holy,
on this celebration of the glorious Virgin Mary.

For at Nazareth she receives with faith
the message of Gabriel
and becomes the Mother of your Son,
begotten by you before the ages,
now born into this world of time
as our Savior and our brother.

At Nazareth too,
in loving communion with her Son,
she watches over the growing Church
in the person of her child
and hands on to us
the shining example of her life.

In the holy house of Nazareth,
as the first disciple of her Son,
she receives the message of the Gospel,
treasures it in her heart,
and reflects on it in her mind.

At Nazareth also this purest of virgins,
united with Joseph, the just man,
in an unbreakable bond of chaste love,
praises you in song,
worships you in silence,
honors you by her daily life,
and gives you glory as she cares for her family.

Now, with all the Saints and Angels,
we praise you for ever:

Holy, Holy, Holy Lord God of hosts . . .

OUR LADY OF CANA P 9

Our Lady Tells the Attendants to do What Her Son Commands

Priest: **The Lord be with you.**
People: **And with your spirit.**

Priest: **Lift up your hearts.**
People: **We lift them up to the Lord.**

Priest: **Let us give thanks to the Lord our God.**
People: **It is right and just.**

**It is truly right to give you thanks,
truly just to give you glory, Father most holy,
on this celebration of the glorious Virgin Mary.**

**For with loving care for the bridegroom and his bride
she turns to her Son for help
and tells the servants to do what he commands.
Water is changed into wine,
the wedding guests rejoice,
as Christ foreshadows the wedding feast
that is his daily gift to his Bride, the Church.**

**In this great sign
the presence of the Messiah is proclaimed,
the outpouring of the Holy Spirit is foretold,
and the hour of salvation is foreshadowed
when Christ will clothe himself
with the royal robes of his Passion
to shed his Blood on the Cross
for his Bride, the Church.**

**Through him the Angels of heaven
offer their prayer of adoration
as they rejoice in your presence for ever.
May our voices be one with theirs
in their triumphant hymn of praise:**

Holy, Holy, Holy Lord God of hosts . . .

MARY, DISCIPLE OF THE LORD P 10

How Blessed Is Mary, Disciple of the Incarnate Word

Priest: **The Lord be with you.**
People: **And with your spirit.**

Priest: **Lift up your hearts.**
People: **We lift them up to the Lord.**

Priest: **Let us give thanks to the Lord our God.**
People: **It is right and just.**

**It is truly right and just, our duty and our salvation,
always and everywhere to give you thanks,
Lord, holy Father, almighty and eternal God,
through Christ our Lord.**

**His Mother, the Virgin Mary in her glory,
is rightly called blessed,
for she received your Son in her virginal womb,
but she is even more blessed
because, as a disciple of the incarnate Word,
she eagerly sought to know your will
and faithfully carried it out.**

**With the whole company of Angels
we praise you with one voice:**

Holy, Holy, Holy Lord God of hosts . . .

MARY AT THE FOOT OF THE CROSS I P 11

Mary Remains Faithful Beside the Cross of Her Son

Priest: **The Lord be with you.**
People: **And with your spirit.**

Priest: **Lift up your hearts.**
People: **We lift them up to the Lord.**

Priest: **Let us give thanks to the Lord our God.**
People: **It is right and just.**

**It is truly right and just, our duty and our salvation,
always and everywhere to give you thanks,
Lord, holy Father, almighty and eternal God,
through Christ our Lord.**

**For in your loving providence
you decreed that Mary, the Mother of your Son,
should stand faithfully beside his Cross,
and so fulfill in her person
the prophecies of old,
and enrich the world
with her own witness of living faith.**

**At the Cross the Blessed Virgin appears as the new Eve,
so that, as a woman shared in bringing death,
so a woman would share in restoring life.**

**At the Cross with motherly love
she embraces her scattered children,
reunited through the Death of Christ,
and she fulfills the mystery of the mother of Zion.**

At the Cross she stands
as the model of the Church, the Bride of Christ,
which draws inspiration from her courage
and keeps constant faith with its Bridegroom,
undaunted by peril and unbroken by persecution.

In our joy we sing to your glory
with all the choirs of Angels:

Holy, Holy, Holy Lord God of hosts . . .

MARY AT THE FOOT OF THE CROSS II P 12

By a Gift of God's Love our Lady Shared in the Passion of Her Son

Priest: **The Lord be with you.**
People: **And with your spirit.**

Priest: **Lift up your hearts.**
People: **We lift them up to the Lord.**

Priest: **Let us give thanks to the Lord our God.**
People: **It is right and just.**

**It is truly right and just, our duty and our salvation,
always and everywhere to give you thanks,
Lord, holy Father, almighty and eternal God,
through Christ our Lord.**

**In your divine wisdom
you planned the redemption of the human race
and decreed that the new Eve
should stand by the Cross of the new Adam:
as she became his Mother
by the power of the Holy Spirit,
so, by a new gift of your love,
she was to be a partner in his Passion,
and she who had given him birth
without the pains of childbirth
was to endure the greatest of pains
in bringing forth to new life
the family of your Church.**

**Now, with Angels and Archangels,
and the whole company of heaven,
we sing the unending hymn of your praise:**

Holy, Holy, Holy Lord God of hosts . . .

THE COMMENDING OF THE BLESSED VIRGIN MARY P 13

Mary and John are Commended to Each Other's Care

Priest: **The Lord be with you.**
People: **And with your spirit.**

Priest: **Lift up your hearts.**
People: **We lift them up to the Lord.**

Priest: **Let us give thanks to the Lord our God.**
People: **It is right and just.**

**It is truly right and just, our duty and our salvation,
always and everywhere to give you thanks,
Lord, holy Father, almighty and eternal God.**

**For at the foot of the Cross of Jesus,
by his solemn and dying wish,
a deep bond of love is fashioned
between the Blessed Virgin Mary
and his faithful disciples:
the Mother of God is entrusted to the disciples
as their own mother,
and they receive her
as a precious inheritance from their Master.**

**She is to be for ever
the mother of those who believe,
and they will look to her
with great confidence in her unfailing protection.
She loves her Son in loving her children,
and in heeding what she says
they keep the words of their Master.**

**Through him the Angels of heaven
offer their prayer of adoration
as they rejoice in your presence for ever.
May our voices be one with theirs
in their triumphant hymn of praise:**

Holy, Holy, Holy Lord God of hosts . . .

MARY, MOTHER OF RECONCILIATION P 14

The Blessed Virgin as the Refuge of Sinners and Mother of Reconciliation

Priest: **The Lord be with you.**
People: **And with your spirit.**

Priest: **Lift up your hearts.**
People: **We lift them up to the Lord.**

Priest: **Let us give thanks to the Lord our God.**
People: **It is right and just.**

**It is truly right and just, almighty and eternal God,
to give you thanks in all things and for all things
and to proclaim your mighty deeds.**

**For in your infinite goodness
you do not abandon those who stray from you,
but in marvelous ways you call them back to your love:
you gave the Blessed Virgin Mary,
sinless as she was,
a heart of compassion for sinners;
seeing her love as their mother,
they turn to her with trust
as they ask your forgiveness;
seeing her beauty of spirit,
they seek to turn away from sin in its ugliness;
taking to heart her words and example,
they learn to keep your Son's commandments.**

**Through him the Angels of heaven
offer their prayer of adoration
as they rejoice in your presence for ever.
May our voices be one with theirs
in their triumphant hymn of praise:**

Holy, Holy, Holy Lord God of hosts . . .

MARY AND THE RESURRECTION OF THE LORD P 15

The Blessed Virgin Looked Forward in Faith to the Resurrection of Her Son

Priest: **The Lord be with you.**
People: **And with your spirit.**

Priest: **Lift up your hearts.**
People: **We lift them up to the Lord.**

Priest: **Let us give thanks to the Lord our God.**
People: **It is right and just.**

**It is truly right and just, our duty and our salvation,
always and everywhere to give you thanks,
Lord, holy Father, almighty and eternal God.**

**For at the Resurrection of your Anointed One
you filled the heart of the Blessed Virgin
with joy beyond all telling
and wonderfully exalted her faith.**

**For it was in faith
that she conceived your Son,
it was in faith
that she awaited his Resurrection.**

**In the strength of faith
she waited for that day of light and life
when the night of death would be ended,
the whole world would exult,
and the infant Church tremble with joy
at seeing again its immortal Lord.**

**Through him the Angels of heaven
offer their prayer of adoration
as they rejoice in your presence for ever.
May our voices be one with theirs
in their triumphant hymn of praise:**

Holy, Holy, Holy Lord God of hosts . . .

MARY, FOUNTAIN OF LIGHT AND LIFE P 16

The Role of the Blessed Virgin in the Sacraments of Christian Initiation

Priest: **The Lord be with you.**
People: **And with your spirit.**

Priest: **Lift up your hearts.**
People: **We lift them up to the Lord.**

Priest: **Let us give thanks to the Lord our God.**
People: **It is right and just.**

**It is truly right and just, our duty and our salvation,
always and everywhere to give you thanks,
Lord, holy Father, almighty and eternal God.**

**By the marvelous gift of your loving kindness
you decreed that the mysteries
accomplished already in the Blessed Virgin
should be accomplished in sign
through the Sacraments of the Church:
for from the baptismal font the Church brings to birth
new sons and daughters conceived in fruitful virginity
through faith and the Holy Spirit.**

**These newborn children the Church anoints
with the precious oil of sacred chrism,
so that the Spirit,
who filled the Blessed Virgin
with an abundance of gifts,
may come down to bless them
with an outpouring of grace.**

Each day the Church also prepares for its children
the table where it nourishes them with the Bread of Heaven,
born of the Virgin Mary for the life of the world:
Jesus Christ our Lord.

Through him the Angels of heaven
offer their prayer of adoration
as they rejoice in your presence for ever.
May our voices be one with theirs
in their triumphant hymn of praise:

Holy, Holy, Holy Lord God of hosts . . .

OUR LADY OF THE CENACLE P 17

The Blessed Virgin, at Prayer with the Apostles, Awaits the Coming of the Paraclete

Priest: **The Lord be with you.**
People: **And with your spirit.**

Priest: **Lift up your hearts.**
People: **We lift them up to the Lord.**

Priest: **Let us give thanks to the Lord our God.**
People: **It is right and just.**

**It is truly right and just, our duty and our salvation,
always and everywhere to give you thanks,
Lord, holy Father, almighty and eternal God.**

**How wonderful is the example you have given us
of harmony and prayer in the Church at its beginning:
you show us the Mother of Jesus
as she prays with the Apostles
in oneness of mind and heart.**

**She who waited in prayer for the coming of Christ
is still at prayer
as she calls upon the promised Paraclete;
she who was overshadowed by the Spirit
at the Incarnation of the Word
is once more filled with your Gift from on high
at the birth of God's new people.**

**As she keeps vigil in prayer,
her heart on fire with love,
she is the model of the Church,
enriched by the gifts of the Spirit
and keeping watch for the Second Coming of Christ.**

Through him the Angels of heaven
offer their prayer of adoration
as they rejoice in your presence for ever.
May our voices be one with theirs
in their triumphant hymn of praise:

Holy, Holy, Holy Lord God of hosts . . .

MARY, QUEEN OF APOSTLES P 18

The Blessed Virgin as Queen of Apostles

Priest: **The Lord be with you.**
People: **And with your spirit.**

Priest: **Lift up your hearts.**
People: **We lift them up to the Lord.**

Priest: **Let us give thanks to the Lord our God.**
People: **It is right and just.**

**It is truly right and just, our duty and our salvation,
always and everywhere to give you thanks,
Lord, holy Father, almighty and eternal God,
on this memorial of the Blessed Virgin Mary,
the first to proclaim Christ,
even before the Apostles.**

**Guided by the Holy Spirit,
she hastened to bring her Son to John,
that he might be sanctified and filled with joy.
It was the same Spirit
who made Peter and the other Apostles
fearless in preaching the Gospel to all nations,
with its saving message of life in Christ.**

**In our own day the Blessed Virgin
inspires by her example new preachers of the Gospel,
cherishes them with a mother's love,
and sustains them by her unceasing prayer,
so that they may bring the Good News of Christ the Savior
to all the world.**

**With all the Saints and Angels
we praise you for ever:**

Holy, Holy, Holy Lord God of hosts . . .

MARY, MOTHER OF THE LORD P 19

The Mother of the Lord Is Entrusted with the Distribution of Divine Grace

Priest: **The Lord be with you.**
People: **And with your spirit.**

Priest: **Lift up your hearts.**
People: **We lift them up to the Lord.**

Priest: **Let us give thanks to the Lord our God.**
People: **It is right and just.**

**It is truly right and just, our duty and our salvation,
always and everywhere to give you thanks,
Lord, holy Father, almighty and eternal God.**

**For in the Mother of your Son
you showed the wonders of your power
and through her you still continue
to accomplish in us our salvation.
In your wisdom and love
she fulfills a mother's role
in the household of the Church
and is entrusted with the distribution of grace.
Through her words you instruct us,
through her example you draw us to follow her Son,
through her prayers you grant us forgiveness.**

**With thankful praise,
in company with the choirs of heaven,
we glorify your power
as we sing with one voice:**

Holy, Holy, Holy Lord God of hosts . . .

MARY, THE NEW EVE P 20

Mary, the New Eve, Is the First Disciple of the New Law

Priest: **The Lord be with you.**
People: **And with your spirit.**

Priest: **Lift up your hearts.**
People: **We lift them up to the Lord.**

Priest: **Let us give thanks to the Lord our God.**
People: **It is right and just.**

**It is truly right and just, our duty and our salvation,
always and everywhere to give you thanks,
Lord, holy Father, almighty and eternal God,
through Christ our Lord.**

**For you gave to Christ, author of the New Covenant,
the Blessed Virgin Mary as his Mother and companion
and you made her the firstfruits of your new people.**

**Conceived without stain,
enriched by gifts of grace,
she is indeed the new woman,
the first disciple of the New Law.**

**She is a woman who finds joy in your service,
who is attentive to the voice of the Spirit,
who is always ready to obey your word.**

**She is a woman blest for her faith,
a woman blest in her child,
a woman raised up from among the lowly.**

**She is a woman standing firm in adversity,
keeping faith by the Cross of her Son,
entering into glory at the end of her days.**

**With the whole company of the Angels
we praise you with one voice:**

Holy, Holy, Holy Lord God of hosts . . .

THE HOLY NAME OF MARY P 21

Our Lady Is the Temple of God's Glory

Priest: **The Lord be with you.**
People: **And with your spirit.**

Priest: **Lift up your hearts.**
People: **We lift them up to the Lord.**

Priest: **Let us give thanks to the Lord our God.**
People: **It is right and just.**

**It is truly right and just, our duty and our salvation,
always and everywhere to give you thanks,
Lord, holy Father, almighty and eternal God,
through Christ our Lord.**

**For in no other name is there salvation;
at his command every knee must bend,
in heaven, on earth, and under the earth.**

**But by your loving providence
the name of the Virgin Mary also
should echo and re-echo
on the lips of your faithful people
who turn to her with confidence
as their star of hope,
call on her as their mother
in time of danger,
and seek her protection
in their hour of need.**

**With thankful praise,
in company with the Angels,
we glorify your power
as we sing with one voice:**

Holy, Holy, Holy Lord God of hosts . . .

MARY, HANDMAID OF THE LORD P 22

The Blessed Virgin, Handmaid of the Lord, Was a Servant of the Mystery of Redemption

Priest: **The Lord be with you.**
People: **And with your spirit.**

Priest: **Lift up your hearts.**
People: **We lift them up to the Lord.**

Priest: **Let us give thanks to the Lord our God.**
People: **It is right and just.**

**It is truly right and just, our duty and our salvation,
always and everywhere to give you thanks,
Lord, holy Father, almighty and eternal God.**

**In the Blessed Virgin Mary
you were especially pleased,
for by embracing your plan of salvation
she gave herself wholeheartedly
to the work of your Son
as a faithful servant of the mystery of redemption.**

**She who gave great service to Christ
was given great honor by you, his Father.
She who saw herself as your lowly handmaid
was raised up by you to reign as queen in glory
in the presence of your Son,
where she intercedes for us in her goodness
as the servant of your love.**

**Now with all the Saints and Angels,
we praise you for ever:**

Holy, Holy, Holy Lord God of hosts . . .

MARY, TEMPLE OF THE LORD P 23

Our Lady Is a Temple of God's Glory Without Compare

Priest: **The Lord be with you.**
People: **And with your spirit.**

Priest: **Lift up your hearts.**
People: **We lift them up to the Lord.**

Priest: **Let us give thanks to the Lord our God.**
People: **It is right and just.**

**It is truly right and just, our duty and our salvation,
always and everywhere to give you thanks,
Lord, holy Father, almighty and eternal God.**

**For by the grace of the Holy Spirit
you purify our hearts by your light
and sanctify them with your presence,
so that they become the dwelling-place of your glory.**

**But because of her obedience of faith
and the mystery of the Incarnation
you made the Blessed Virgin your temple without compare:
a house of gold adorned by the Spirit
with every kind of virtue,
a royal palace resplendent
with the presence of the One who is the Truth,
the holy city, rejoicing in its streams of grace,
the ark of the New Covenant
enshrining the author of the New Law,
Jesus Christ our Lord.**

**Through him the Angels of heaven
offer their prayer of adoration
as they rejoice in your presence for ever.
May our voices be one with theirs
in their triumphant hymn of praise:**

Holy, Holy, Holy Lord God of hosts . . .

MARY, SEAT OF WISDOM P 24

Wisdom Has Built Himself a House in the Chaste Womb of Mary

Priest: **The Lord be with you.**
People: **And with your spirit.**

Priest: **Lift up your hearts.**
People: **We lift them up to the Lord.**

Priest: **Let us give thanks to the Lord our God.**
People: **It is right and just.**

**It is truly right and just, our duty and our salvation,
always and everywhere to give you thanks,
Lord, holy Father, almighty and eternal God,
through Christ our Lord.**

**For in your infinite goodness,
when the fullness of time had come,
you accomplished through the Blessed Virgin Mary
the mystery of our reconciliation planned before all ages.
Wisdom built himself a house
in the chaste womb of the Virgin Mary,
the Creator of time came to be born
in this world of time,
so that as the new Adam
he might undo the ancient inheritance of sin
and renew us in his own resplendent image.**

**With all the Saints and Angels
we praise you for ever:**

Holy, Holy, Holy Lord God of hosts . . .

MARY, IMAGE AND MOTHER OF THE CHURCH I P 25

Mary Is the Image and Mother of the Church

Priest: **The Lord be with you.**
People: **And with your spirit.**

Priest: **Lift up your hearts.**
People: **We lift them up to the Lord.**

Priest: **Let us give thanks to the Lord our God.**
People: **It is right and just.**

**It is truly right and just, our duty and our salvation,
always and everywhere to give you thanks,
Lord, holy Father, almighty and eternal God,
and to proclaim your greatness with due praise,
as we honor the Blessed Virgin Mary.**

**Receiving your Word in her Immaculate Heart,
she was found worthy to conceive him in her virgin's womb
and, giving birth to the Creator,
she nurtured the beginnings of the Church.**

**Standing beside the Cross,
she received the testament of divine love
and took to herself as sons and daughters
all those who by the Death of Christ
are born to heavenly life.**

**As the Apostles awaited the Spirit you had promised,
she joined her supplication to the prayers of the disciples
and so became the pattern of the Church at prayer.**

**Raised to the glory of heaven,
she accompanies your pilgrim Church with a mother's love
and watches in kindness over the Church's homeward steps,
until the Lord's Day shall come in glorious splendor.**

**And so, with all the Angels and Saints,
we praise you, as without end we acclaim:**

Holy, Holy, Holy Lord God of hosts . . .

MARY, IMAGE AND MOTHER OF THE CHURCH II P 26

Our Lady as an Example of True Worship

Priest: **The Lord be with you.**
People: **And with your spirit.**

Priest: **Lift up your hearts.**
People: **We lift them up to the Lord.**

Priest: **Let us give thanks to the Lord our God.**
People: **It is right and just.**

**It is truly right and just, our duty and our salvation,
always and everywhere to give you thanks,
Lord, holy Father, almighty and eternal God,
through Christ our Lord.**

**For in your infinite goodness
you have given to the virgin Church
the model of true worship in the Virgin Mary.**

**She is the Virgin who listens,
who embraces your words with joy,
treasuring them in the silence of her heart.**

**She is the Virgin of prayer,
who sings of your mercy in her canticle of praise,
who shows concern for the bridegroom and bride of Cana
and intercedes for them with her Son,
who prays with the Apostles in oneness of mind and heart.**

**She is the Virgin Mother,
who gives birth to your Son
by the power of the Holy Spirit
and at the foot of the Cross
is proclaimed as mother
of the people of the New Covenant.**

**She is the Virgin who offers,
presenting the Firstborn in your temple
and sharing in his self-offering
beside the tree of everlasting life.**

**She is the Virgin who keeps vigil,
awaiting the Resurrection of her Son
with unwavering hope
and looking forward to the coming of the Holy Spirit,
with steadfast faith.**

**In our joy we sing to your glory
with all the choirs of Angels:**

Holy, Holy, Holy Lord God of hosts . . .

MARY, IMAGE AND MOTHER OF THE CHURCH III P 27

The Blessed Virgin Is the Resplendent Image of the Church in Its Future Glory

Priest: **The Lord be with you.**
People: **And with your spirit.**

Priest: **Lift up your hearts.**
People: **We lift them up to the Lord.**

Priest: **Let us give thanks to the Lord our God.**
People: **It is right and just.**

**It is truly right and just, our duty and our salvation,
always and everywhere to give you thanks,
Lord, holy Father, almighty and eternal God.**

**For you have given the Blessed Virgin Mary to your Church
as the perfect image of its role as mother
and of its future glory.**

**She is a virgin unsurpassed in purity of faith,
a bride joined to Christ
in an unbreakable bond of love
and united with him in his suffering.**

**She is a mother by the overshadowing of the Holy Spirit,
filled with loving concern for all her children.**

**She is a queen adorned with the jewels of grace,
robed with the sun and crowned with stars,
sharing eternally in the glory of her Lord.**

**Through him the Angels of heaven
offer their prayer of adoration
as they rejoice in your presence for ever.
May our voices be one with theirs
in their triumphant hymn of praise:**

Holy, Holy, Holy Lord God of hosts . . .

THE IMMACULATE HEART OF MARY P 28

The Heart of Mary Is the Heart of One Who Lives By the New Law

Priest: **The Lord be with you.**
People: **And with your spirit.**

Priest: **Lift up your hearts.**
People: **We lift them up to the Lord.**

Priest: **Let us give thanks to the Lord our God.**
People: **It is right and just.**

**It is truly right and just, our duty and our salvation,
always and everywhere to give you thanks,
Lord, holy Father, almighty and eternal God,
through Christ our Lord.**

**For you gave the Blessed Virgin Mary
a wise and obedient heart,
that she might perfectly carry out your will,
a new and gentle heart,
in which you were well pleased
and on which you inscribed
the law of the New Covenant.**

**You gave her an undivided and pure heart,
that she might be worthy
to be the Virgin Mother of your Son
and to rejoice to see you for ever.**

**You gave her a steadfast and watchful heart,
so that she could endure without fear the sword of sorrow
and await in faith the Resurrection of her Son.**

**With the whole company of the Angels
we sing your praises
in their canticle of joy:**

Holy, Holy, Holy Lord God of hosts . . .

MARY, QUEEN OF ALL CREATION P 29

The Lowly Handmaid of the Lord Is Exalted as Queen of Heaven

Priest: **The Lord be with you.**
People: **And with your spirit.**

Priest: **Lift up your hearts.**
People: **We lift them up to the Lord.**

Priest: **Let us give thanks to the Lord our God.**
People: **It is right and just.**

It is truly right and just, our duty and our salvation,
always and everywhere to give you thanks,
Lord, holy Father, almighty and eternal God,
through Christ our Lord.

For you are merciful and just,
scattering the proud and raising up the broken-hearted.
When your Son humbled himself and accepted death
you crowned him with glory and honor
and seated him at your right hand
as King of kings and Lord of lords.

When the Blessed Virgin, your lowly handmaid,
endured with patient suffering
the shame of her Son's Crucifixion
you exalted her above all the choirs of Angels
to reign with him in glory
and to intercede for all your children,
our advocate of grace
and the queen of all creation.

With the whole host of Angels
we proclaim your greatness
as we praise you with one voice:

Holy, Holy, Holy Lord God of hosts . . .

MARY, MOTHER AND MEDIATRIX OF GRACE P 30

The Love the Blessed Virgin Bestows as a Mother

Priest: **The Lord be with you.**
People: **And with your spirit.**

Priest: **Lift up your hearts.**
People: **We lift them up to the Lord.**

Priest: **Let us give thanks to the Lord our God.**
People: **It is right and just.**

**It is truly right and just, our duty and our salvation,
always and everywhere to give you thanks,
Lord, holy Father, almighty and eternal God,
through Christ our Lord.**

**For truly God and truly human,
he was chosen by you as
the one Mediator between you
and the human family,
always living to make intercession for us.**

**In your wisdom and goodness
the Blessed Virgin Mary, the Mother and companion of
the Redeemer,
was to have a maternal role in the Church:
of intercession and pardon,
of prayer and grace,
of reconciliation and peace.**

**The love that she bestows as a mother
is entirely the gift of Christ, the one Mediator,
from whom alone she receives her power.**

**Her children, in their trials and fears,
turn with confidence to the Blessed Virgin,
calling to her as Mother of mercy and handmaid of grace.**

**In our joy we sing to your glory
with all the choirs of Angels:**

Holy, Holy, Holy Lord God of hosts . . .

MARY, FOUNTAIN OF SALVATION P 31

The Blessed Virgin Brought Forth Jesus Christ, the Fountain of Living Water

Priest: **The Lord be with you.**
People: **And with your spirit.**

Priest: **Lift up your hearts.**
People: **We lift them up to the Lord.**

Priest: **Let us give thanks to the Lord our God.**
People: **It is right and just.**

It is truly right and just, our duty and our salvation,
always and everywhere to give you thanks,
Lord, holy Father, and, as we celebrate the glory of the Blessed Virgin Mary,
to proclaim with fitting praise
the greatness of your name.

In the great mystery of the Incarnation
the Holy Spirit overshadowed the Blessed Virgin
and she brought forth your eternal Word,
Jesus Christ, the fountain of living water,
from which all may satisfy their thirst
to be one with you in a communion of love.

The Church also provided for all the faithful
the waters flowing from Christ's side.
These are the rich, life-giving waters
served in the Sacraments,
so that those who share in them with faith
may be filled with the Holy Spirit
and may find Christ, their Savior.

Through him the Angels of heaven
offer their prayer of adoration
as they rejoice in your presence for ever.
May our voices be one with theirs
in their triumphant hymn of praise:

Holy, Holy, Holy Lord God of hosts . . .

MARY, MOTHER AND TEACHER IN THE SPIRIT P 32

The Blessed Virgin, our Mother, Lovingly Encourages Her Children and Guides Them by Her Example

Priest: **The Lord be with you.**
People: **And with your spirit.**

Priest: **Lift up your hearts.**
People: **We lift them up to the Lord.**

Priest: **Let us give thanks to the Lord our God.**
People: **It is right and just.**

**It is truly right and just, our duty and our salvation,
always and everywhere to give you thanks,
Lord, holy Father, almighty and eternal God,
and, as we celebrate the memory of Blessed Mary ever-Virgin,
to praise, to bless, and to proclaim your holy name.**

**So intimately does she share in the mystery of Christ
that she is still a mother,
continuing to give you children with the Church,
encouraging them by her love,
and drawing them by her example
to pursue perfect charity.**

**She is the model
of all who live by the spirit of the Gospel;
as we look up to her in prayer
we learn from her mind
to love you above all things,
from her spirit
to be rapt in contemplation of your Word,
and from her heart
to serve the needs of others.**

**In our joy we sing to your glory
with all the choirs of Angels:**

Holy, Holy, Holy Lord God of hosts . . .

MARY, MOTHER OF GOOD COUNSEL P 33

Our Lady Gave Herself Wholeheartedly to God's Loving Plan

Priest: **The Lord be with you.**
People: **And with your spirit.**

Priest: **Lift up your hearts.**
People: **We lift them up to the Lord.**

Priest: **Let us give thanks to the Lord our God.**
People: **It is right and just.**

**It is truly right and just, our duty and our salvation,
always and everywhere to give you thanks,
Lord, holy Father, almighty and eternal God,
through Christ our Lord.**

**How generously you poured out
the gifts of your Holy Spirit
upon the Blessed Virgin Mary
to make her worthy
to be the Mother and companion of the Redeemer.**

**Enlightened by these gifts,
she sought your will unceasingly
and obeyed it with fidelity.
In her canticle of joy
she proclaimed the greatness of your mercy
and gave herself wholeheartedly
to your wise and loving plan
for renewing all things in Christ.**

**Through him the Angels of heaven
offer their prayer of adoration
as they rejoice in your presence for ever.
May our voices be one with theirs
in their triumphant hymn of praise:**

Holy, Holy, Holy Lord God of hosts . . .

MARY, CAUSE OF OUR JOY P 34

The Life of the Blessed Virgin, Cause of Our Joy

Priest: **The Lord be with you.**
People: **And with your spirit.**

Priest: **Lift up your hearts.**
People: **We lift them up to the Lord.**

Priest: **Let us give thanks to the Lord our God.**
People: **It is right and just.**

It is truly right and just, our duty and our salvation,
always and everywhere to give you thanks,
Lord, holy Father, and, as we honor the memory of the Blessed Virgin,
the daughter of your love,
to proclaim with fitting praise
the greatness of your name.

Her blessed birth
heralded joy for all the world.
Her virgin-motherhood
brought forth the true Light,
the source of all joy.
Her hidden life
brings light and warmth
to all the Churches of the world.
Her passing into glory
raised her to the heights of heaven,
where, as our sister and our Mother,
she waits for us with loving care
until we too enjoy the vision of your glory for ever.

In our joy we sing to your glory
with all the choirs of Angels:

Holy, Holy, Holy Lord God of hosts . . .

MARY, PILLAR OF FAITH P 35

Our Lady Is the Hope of the Faithful, a Pillar of Faith

Priest: **The Lord be with you.**
People: **And with your spirit.**

Priest: **Lift up your hearts.**
People: **We lift them up to the Lord.**

Priest: **Let us give thanks to the Lord our God.**
People: **It is right and just.**

**It is truly right and just, our duty and our salvation,
always and everywhere to give you thanks,
Lord, holy Father, for the many wonders of love and grace
poured out upon the Blessed Virgin Mary
by your loving kindness.**

**You kept her untouched
by the stain of original sin
and the corruption of the grave.
Spotless in her virginity,
she became the fitting shrine
from which Christ was born
to be revealed as the light of the nations
and the Bridegroom of the Church.
Bathed in the glory of her Son,
she shines upon his people
as a star of hope and a pillar of faith.**

**In our unending joy we echo on earth
the song of the Angels in heaven
as they praise your glory for ever:**

Holy, Holy, Holy Lord God of hosts . . .

MARY, MOTHER OF FAIREST LOVE P 36

Mary Is All-Beautiful

Priest: **The Lord be with you.**
People: **And with your spirit.**

Priest: **Lift up your hearts.**
People: **We lift them up to the Lord.**

Priest: **Let us give thanks to the Lord our God.**
People: **It is right and just.**

**It is truly right and just, our duty and our salvation,
always and everywhere to give you thanks,
Lord, holy Father, and, as we celebrate the memory of the Blessed Virgin Mary,
to proclaim with fitting praise
the greatness of your name.**

**Beauty was hers at her conception:
free from all stain of sin,
she is resplendent in the glory of grace.**

**Beauty was hers in her virginal motherhood:
she brought forth her Son, the radiance of your glory,
as the Savior and brother of us all.**

**Beauty was hers in the Passion of her Son:
marked by his Blood,
in her meekness she shared the suffering
of the Lamb of God, her Son, silent before his executioners,
and won for herself a new title of motherhood.**

**Beauty was hers in the Resurrection of Christ:
she reigns with him in glory,
the sharer now in his triumph.**

Through him the Angels of heaven
offer their prayer of adoration
as they rejoice in your presence for ever.
May our voices be one with theirs
in their triumphant hymn of praise:

Holy, Holy, Holy Lord God of hosts . . .

MARY, MOTHER OF DIVINE HOPE P 37

Mary Is an Example of Hope in God

Priest: **The Lord be with you.**
People: **And with your spirit.**

Priest: **Lift up your hearts.**
People: **We lift them up to the Lord.**

Priest: **Let us give thanks to the Lord our God.**
People: **It is right and just.**

**It is truly right and just, our duty and our salvation,
to give you thanks with all our hearts, Lord, holy Father,
for your gift to our human family
of Jesus Christ, the author of our salvation,
and of Mary, his Mother, the model of divine hope.**

**Your lowly handmaid
placed all her trust in you:
she awaited in hope
and conceived in faith the Son of Man,
whom the prophets had foretold.**

**With untiring love
she gave herself to his service
and became the Mother of all the living.**

**Mary, the fairest fruit of Christ's redeeming love,
is a sister to all the children of Adam
as they journey toward the fullness of freedom
and raise their eyes to her,
the sign of sure hope and comfort,
until the day of the Lord dawns in glory.**

**In our joy we sing
with all the choirs of Angels:**

Holy, Holy, Holy Lord God of hosts . . .

MARY, MOTHER OF UNITY P 38

The Role of the Blessed Virgin in Fostering the Unity of the Church

Priest: **The Lord be with you.**
People: **And with your spirit.**

Priest: **Lift up your hearts.**
People: **We lift them up to the Lord.**

Priest: **Let us give thanks to the Lord our God.**
People: **It is right and just.**

**It is truly right and just, our duty and our salvation,
always and everywhere to give you thanks,
Lord, holy Father, almighty and eternal God,
through Christ our Lord.**

**For he is the one who makes whole,
the lover of unity,
who chose for his Mother
a woman unstained in heart and body,
and for his Bride
the one and undivided Church.**

**Lifted high above the earth,
in the presence of his Mother,
he gathered your scattered children into unity,
joining them to himself
with bonds of love.**

**Returning to you
and seated at your right hand,
he sent upon the Blessed Virgin,
at prayer with the Apostles,
the Spirit of concord and unity,
of peace and forgiveness.**

**We praise you, Lord,
with all the Angels and Saints in their song of joy:**

Holy, Holy, Holy Lord God of hosts . . .

MARY, QUEEN AND MOTHER OF MERCY P 39

The Blessed Virgin Is Queen of Pity and Mother of Mercy

Priest: **The Lord be with you.**
People: **And with your spirit.**

Priest: **Lift up your hearts.**
People: **We lift them up to the Lord.**

Priest: **Let us give thanks to the Lord our God.**
People: **It is right and just.**

**It is truly right and just, our duty and our salvation,
always and everywhere to give you thanks,
Lord, holy Father, and, as we celebrate the memory of the Blessed Virgin Mary,
to proclaim with fitting praise
the greatness of your name.**

**She is the gracious queen
who has herself uniquely known your loving kindness
and stretches out her arms
to embrace all who take refuge in her
and call upon her help in their distress.**

**She is the Mother of mercy,
always attentive to the voice of her children,
seeking to win your compassion for them,
and asking your forgiveness for their sins.**

**She is the handmaid of your love,
never ceasing to pray for us to your Son,
that he may enrich our poverty with his grace
and strengthen our weakness with his power.**

**Through him the Angels of heaven
offer their prayer of adoration
as they rejoice in your presence for ever.
May our voices be one with theirs
in their triumphant hymn of praise:**

Holy, Holy, Holy Lord God of hosts . . .

MARY, MOTHER OF DIVINE PROVIDENCE P 40

The Blessed Virgin Is the Handmaid of God's Love and a Generous Mother to Her Children

Priest: **The Lord be with you.**
People: **And with your spirit.**

Priest: **Lift up your hearts.**
People: **We lift them up to the Lord.**

Priest: **Let us give thanks to the Lord our God.**
People: **It is right and just.**

**It is truly right and just, our duty and our salvation,
always and everywhere to give you thanks,
Lord, holy Father, almighty and eternal God,
through Christ our Lord.**

**For in the wisdom of your providence
the Blessed Virgin Mary was overshadowed by the Holy Spirit
and gave birth to the Savior of the world.**

**In Cana of Galilee,
when she interceded with her Son
for the bridegroom and bride,
he gave the first of his signs:
water was turned into wine,
the wedding guests rejoiced,
and the disciples believed in their Master.**

**Now, enthroned as queen at her Son's right hand,
she provides for all the needs of the Church
as the handmaid of your love
and as a mother who cares for each of her children,
entrusted to her by Christ Jesus
while he hung upon the Cross.**

**Now with all the Saints and Angels,
we praise you for ever:**

Holy, Holy, Holy Lord God of hosts . . .

MARY, MOTHER OF CONSOLATION P 41

The Blessed Virgin, Consoled by the Lord, in Her Turn Consoles Her Children

Priest: **The Lord be with you.**
People: **And with your spirit.**

Priest: **Lift up your hearts.**
People: **We lift them up to the Lord.**

Priest: **Let us give thanks to the Lord our God.**
People: **It is right and just.**

It is truly right and just to give you thanks,
and to bless and praise you, almighty and eternal God,
through Christ our Lord.

He was received with joy by the Blessed Virgin
and brought to birth from her chaste womb
as the consolation of the world.

As she endured her bitter agony
at the Cross of her Son,
she was consoled by you
with the hope of his Resurrection.

In company with the Apostles
she earnestly prayed and awaited with trust
the coming of the Spirit of consolation and peace.

Now, assumed into heaven,
she consoles with a mother's love
all who turn to her with faith,
until the day of the Lord dawns in glory.

Now with all the Saints and Angels,
we praise you for ever:

Holy, Holy, Holy Lord God of hosts . . .

MARY, HELP OF CHRISTIANS P 42

The Blessed Virgin as the Mother and Help of Christians

Priest: **The Lord be with you.**
People: **And with your spirit.**

Priest: **Lift up your hearts.**
People: **We lift them up to the Lord.**

Priest: **Let us give thanks to the Lord our God.**
People: **It is right and just.**

It is truly right and just, our duty and our salvation,
always and everywhere to give you thanks,
Lord, holy Father, almighty and eternal God,
through Christ our Lord.

For you chose the Immaculate Virgin Mary,
the Mother of your Son,
to be the Mother and help of Christians,
so that under her protection
we might be fearless in waging the battle of faith,
steadfast in holding the teaching of the Apostles,
and tranquil in spirit in the storms of this world,
until we reach the joy of your heavenly city.

With steadfast love
we sing your unending praise;
we join with the hosts of heaven
in their triumphant song:

Holy, Holy, Holy Lord God of hosts . . .

OUR LADY OF RANSOM P 43

Holy Mary as Mother of the Redeemer and Handmaid of Redemption

Priest: **The Lord be with you.**
People: **And with your spirit.**

Priest: **Lift up your hearts.**
People: **We lift them up to the Lord.**

Priest: **Let us give thanks to the Lord our God.**
People: **It is right and just.**

It is truly right and just, our duty and our salvation,
always and everywhere to give you thanks,
Lord, holy Father, almighty and eternal God.

For in your wise and provident plan
you joined the Blessed Virgin
so closely to your Son
in the work of redemption
that she was with him
as a loving mother in his infancy,
stood by his Cross
as the faithful companion in his Passion,
and, assumed into heaven,
became our advocate,
and the handmaid of our redemption.

She cares unceasingly with a mother's love
for all your children in their need,
breaking the chains of every form of captivity,
that they might enjoy full liberty of body and spirit.

Now, with the Angels and all the Saints
we praise the redeeming love of your Son
and through him we proclaim your greatness,
as we cry out with one voice:

Holy, Holy, Holy Lord God of hosts . . .

MARY, HEALTH OF THE SICK P 44

The Blessed Virgin Is a Sign of Salvation for the Sick

Priest: **The Lord be with you.**
People: **And with your spirit.**

Priest: **Lift up your hearts.**
People: **We lift them up to the Lord.**

Priest: **Let us give thanks to the Lord our God.**
People: **It is right and just.**

**It is truly right and just, our duty and our salvation,
always and everywhere to give you thanks,
Lord, holy Father, almighty and eternal God.**

**For in a wonderful way you gave the Blessed Virgin Mary
a special share in the mystery of pain.
She now shines radiantly
as a sign of health, of healing, and of divine hope
for the sick who call on her patronage.**

**To all who look up to her in prayer
she is the model of perfect acceptance of your will
and of wholehearted conformity with Christ,
who, out of love for us,
endured our weakness
and bore our sufferings.**

**Through Christ the Angels of heaven
offer their prayer of adoration
as they rejoice in your presence for ever.
May our voices be one with theirs
in their triumphant hymn of praise:**

Holy, Holy, Holy Lord God of hosts . . .

MARY, QUEEN OF PEACE P 45

The Mother of Christ Is Daughter and Queen of Peace

Priest: **The Lord be with you.**
People: **And with your spirit.**

Priest: **Lift up your hearts.**
People: **We lift them up to the Lord.**

Priest: **Let us give thanks to the Lord our God.**
People: **It is right and just.**

It is truly right and just, our duty and our salvation,
always and everywhere to give you thanks,
Lord, holy Father, and, as we honor the memory of the Blessed Virgin Mary,
to proclaim with fitting praise
the greatness of your name.

She is your lowly handmaid,
receiving your word from the Angel Gabriel
and conceiving in her virginal womb
the Prince of Peace, Jesus Christ,
your Son, our Lord.

She is the faithful Mother,
standing fearless beside the Cross
as her Son sheds his Blood for our salvation
and reconciles all things to himself in peace.

She is the disciple of Christ and daughter of peace,
joining in prayer with the Apostles
as she awaits your promised Gift,
the Spirit of unity and peace, of love and joy.

Now, with the Saints and all the Angels
we praise you for ever:

Holy, Holy, Holy Lord God of hosts . . .

MARY, GATE OF HEAVEN P 46

The Gate Closed by Eve has been Reopened by the Blessed Virgin

Priest: **The Lord be with you.**
People: **And with your spirit.**

Priest: **Lift up your hearts.**
People: **We lift them up to the Lord.**

Priest: **Let us give thanks to the Lord our God.**
People: **It is right and just.**

It is truly right and just, our duty and our salvation,
always and everywhere to give you thanks,
Lord, holy Father, and to praise and bless your holy name
as we celebrate the memory of the Blessed Virgin Mary.

She is the Virgin Mother,
prefigured in the eastern gate of the temple,
through which the Lord would enter,
and after him no other.

She is the humble Virgin,
whose faith opened the gate of eternal life,
closed by the disbelief of Eve.

She is the Virgin at prayer,
always interceding for sinners
that they may turn to her Son,
who unseals the fountain of ever-flowing grace
and opens the door of forgiveness.

Through him the Angels of heaven
offer their prayer of adoration
as they rejoice in your presence for ever.
May our voices be one with theirs
in their triumphant hymn of praise:

Holy, Holy, Holy Lord God of hosts . . .

BLESSED VIRGIN MARY I P 47

The Motherhood of the Blessed Virgin Mary

Priest: **The Lord be with you.**
People: **And with your spirit.**

Priest: **Lift up your hearts.**
People: **We lift them up to the Lord.**

Priest: **Let us give thanks to the Lord our God.**
People: **It is right and just.**

**It is truly right and just, our duty and our salvation,
always and everywhere to give you thanks,
Lord, holy Father, almighty and eternal God,
and to praise, bless, and glorify your name
(on the Solemnity of the Motherhood /
on the feast day / on the Nativity / in veneration)
of the Blessed ever-Virgin Mary.**

**For by the overshadowing of the Holy Spirit
she conceived your Only Begotten Son,
and without losing the glory of virginity,
brought forth into the world the eternal Light,
Jesus Christ our Lord.**

**Through him the Angels praise your majesty
Dominons adore and Powers tremble before you.
Heaven and the Virtues of heaven and the blessed Seraphim
worship together with exultation.
May our voices, we pray, join with theirs
in humble praise, as we acclaim:**

Holy, Holy, Holy Lord God of hosts . . .

BLESSED VIRGIN MARY II P 48

The Church Praises God with the Words of Mary

Priest: **The Lord be with you.**
People: **And with your spirit.**

Priest: **Lift up your hearts.**
People: **We lift them up to the Lord.**

Priest: **Let us give thanks to the Lord our God.**
People: **It is right and just.**

It is truly right and just, our duty and our salvation,
to praise your mighty deeds in the exaltation of all the Saints,
and especially, as we celebrate the memory of the Blessed Virgin Mary,
to proclaim your kindness as we echo her thankful hymn of praise.

For truly even to earth's ends you have done great things
and extended your abundant mercy from age to age:
when you looked on the lowliness of your handmaid,
you gave us through the author of our salvation,
your Son, Jesus Christ, our Lord.

Through him the host of Angels adores your majesty
and rejoices in your presence for ever.
May our voices, we pray, join with theirs
in one chorus of exultant praise, as we acclaim:

Holy, Holy, Holy Lord God of hosts . . .

IMMACULATE CONCEPTION P 49

The Mystery of Mary and the Church

Priest: **The Lord be with you.**
People: **And with your spirit.**

Priest: **Lift up your hearts.**
People: **We lift them up to the Lord.**

Priest: **Let us give thanks to the Lord our God.**
People: **It is right and just.**

It is truly right and just, our duty and our salvation,
always and everywhere to give you thanks,
Lord, holy Father, almighty and eternal God.

For you preserved the most Blessed Virgin Mary
from all stain of original sin,
so that in her, endowed with the rich fullness of your grace,
you might prepare a worthy Mother for your Son
and signify the beginning of the Church,
his beautiful Bride without spot or wrinkle.

She, the most pure Virgin, was to bring forth a Son,
the innocent Lamb who would wipe away our offenses;
you placed her above all others
to be for your people an advocate of grace
and a model of holiness.

And so, in company with the choirs of Angels,
we praise you, and with joy we proclaim:

Holy, Holy, Holy Lord God of hosts . . .

ASSUMPTION P 50

The Glory of Mary Assumed into Heaven

Priest: **The Lord be with you.**
People: **And with your spirit.**

Priest: **Lift up your hearts.**
People: **We lift them up to the Lord.**

Priest: **Let us give thanks to the Lord our God.**
People: **It is right and just.**

**It is truly right and just, our duty and our salvation,
always and everywhere to give you thanks,
Lord, holy Father, almighty and eternal God,
through Christ our Lord.**

**For today the Virgin Mother of God
was assumed into heaven
as the beginning and image
of your Church's coming to perfection
and a sign of sure hope and comfort to your pilgrim people;
rightly you would not allow her
to see the corruption of the tomb
since from her own body she marvelously brought forth
your incarnate Son, the Author of all life.**

**And so, in company with choirs of Angels,
we praise you, and with joy we proclaim:**

Holy, Holy, Holy Lord God of hosts . . .

EUCHARISTIC PRAYER I
(THE ROMAN CANON)

83. ℣. **The Lord be with you.**
℟. And with your spirit.

℣. **Lift up your hearts.**
℟. We lift them up to the Lord.

℣. **Let us give thanks to the Lord our God.**
℟. It is right and just.

Then follows the Preface to be used in accord with the rubrics, which concludes:

Holy, Holy, Holy Lord God of hosts.
Heaven and earth are full of your glory.
Hosanna in the highest.
Blessed is he who comes in the name of the Lord.
Hosanna in the highest.

84. The Priest, with hands extended, says:

To you, therefore, most merciful Father, Celebrant alone
we make humble prayer and petition
through Jesus Christ, your Son, our Lord:

He joins his hands and says

that you accept

He makes the Sign of the Cross once over the bread and chalice together, saying:

and bless ✠ these gifts, these offerings,
these holy and unblemished sacrifices,

With hands extended, he continues:

which we offer you firstly
for your holy catholic Church.
Be pleased to grant her peace,
to guard, unite and govern her
throughout the whole world,
together with your servant N. our Pope
and N. our Bishop,*

* Mention may be made here of the Coadjutor Bishop, or Auxiliary Bishops, as noted in the *General Instruction of the Roman Missal*, no. 149.

and all those who, holding to the truth,
hand on the catholic and apostolic faith.

85. Commemoration of the Living.

Celebrant or one concelebrant

Remember, Lord, your servants N. **and** N.

The Priest joins his hands and prays briefly for those for whom he intends to pray.

Then, with hands extended, he continues:

and all gathered here,
whose faith and devotion are known to you.
For them, we offer you this sacrifice of praise
or they offer it for themselves
and all who are dear to them:
for the redemption of their souls,
in hope of health and well-being,
and paying their homage to you,
the eternal God, living and true.

86. Within the Action.

Celebrant or one concelebrant

In communion with those whose memory we venerate,
especially the glorious ever-Virgin Mary,
Mother of our God and Lord, Jesus Christ,
† **and blessed Joseph, her Spouse,**
your blessed Apostles and Martyrs,
Peter and Paul, Andrew,
(**James, John,**
Thomas, James, Philip,
Bartholomew, Matthew,
Simon and Jude;
Linus, Cletus, Clement, Sixtus,
Cornelius, Cyprian,
Lawrence, Chrysogonus,
John and Paul,
Cosmas and Damian)
and all your Saints;
we ask that through their merits and prayers,
in all things we may be defended
by your protecting help.
(**Through Christ our Lord. Amen.**)

87. With hands extended, the Priest continues:

Celebrant alone

Therefore, Lord, we pray:
graciously accept this oblation of our service,
that of your whole family;
order our days in your peace,
and command that we be delivered from eternal damnation
and counted among the flock of those you have chosen.

He joins his hands.

(Through Christ our Lord. Amen.)

88. Holding his hands extended over the offerings, he says:

Celebrant with concelebrants

Be pleased, O God, we pray,
to bless, acknowledge,
and approve this offering in every respect;
make it spiritual and acceptable,
so that it may become for us
the Body and Blood of your most beloved Son,
our Lord Jesus Christ.

He joins his hands.

89. In the formulas that follow, the words of the Lord should be pronounced clearly and distinctly, as the nature of these words requires.

On the day before he was to suffer,

He takes the bread
and, holding it slightly raised above the altar, continues:

he took bread in his holy and venerable hands,

He raises his eyes.

and with eyes raised to heaven
to you, O God, his almighty Father,
giving you thanks, he said the blessing,
broke the bread
and gave it to his disciples, saying:

He bows slightly.

TAKE THIS, ALL OF YOU, AND EAT OF IT,
FOR THIS IS MY BODY,
WHICH WILL BE GIVEN UP FOR YOU.

He shows the consecrated host to the people, places it again on the paten, and genuflects in adoration.

90. After this, the Priest continues:

In a similar way, when supper was ended,

He takes the chalice
and, holding it slightly raised above the altar, continues:

he took this precious chalice
in his holy and venerable hands,
and once more giving you thanks, he said the blessing
and gave the chalice to his disciples, saying:

He bows slightly.

TAKE THIS, ALL OF YOU, AND DRINK FROM IT,
FOR THIS IS THE CHALICE OF MY BLOOD,
THE BLOOD OF THE NEW AND ETERNAL COVENANT,
WHICH WILL BE POURED OUT FOR YOU AND FOR MANY
FOR THE FORGIVENESS OF SINS.

DO THIS IN MEMORY OF ME.

He shows the chalice to the people, places it on the corporal, and genuflects in adoration.

91. Then he says:

Or:

The mystery of faith. Celebrant alone

And the people continue, acclaiming:

We proclaim your Death, O Lord,
and profess your Resurrection
until you come again.

Or:

When we eat this Bread and drink this Cup,
we proclaim your Death, O Lord,
until you come again.

Or:

Save us, Savior of the world,
for by your Cross and Resurrection
you have set us free.

92. Then the Priest, with hands extended, says:

Celebrant with concelebrants

**Therefore, O Lord,
as we celebrate the memorial of the blessed Passion,
the Resurrection from the dead,
and the glorious Ascension into heaven
of Christ, your Son, our Lord,
we, your servants and your holy people,
offer to your glorious majesty
from the gifts that you have given us,
this pure victim,
this holy victim,
this spotless victim,
the holy Bread of eternal life
and the Chalice of everlasting salvation.**

93. **Be pleased to look upon these offerings
with a serene and kindly countenance,
and to accept them,
as once you were pleased to accept
the gifts of your servant Abel the just,
the sacrifice of Abraham, our father in faith,**

and the offering of your high priest Melchizedek,
a holy sacrifice, a spotless victim.

94. Bowing, with hands joined, he continues:

In humble prayer we ask you, almighty God:
command that these gifts be borne
by the hands of your holy Angel
to your altar on high
in the sight of your divine majesty,
so that all of us, who through this participation at the altar
receive the most holy Body and Blood of your Son,

He stands upright again and signs himself with the Sign of the Cross, saying:

may be filled with every grace and heavenly blessing.

He joins his hands.

(Through Christ our Lord. Amen.)

95. Commemoration of the Dead

With hands extended, the Priest says:

Celebrant or one concelebrant

Remember also, Lord, your servants N. and N.,
who have gone before us with the sign of faith
and rest in the sleep of peace.

He joins his hands and prays briefly for those who have died and for whom he intends to pray.

Then, with hands extended, he continues:

Grant them, O Lord, we pray,
and all who sleep in Christ,
a place of refreshment, light and peace.

He joins his hands.

(Through Christ our Lord. Amen.)

96. He strikes his breast with his right hand, saying:

Celebrant or one concelebrant

To us, also, your servants, who, though sinners,

And, with hands extended, he continues:

hope in your abundant mercies,
graciously grant some share
and fellowship with your holy Apostles and Martyrs:
with John the Baptist, Stephen,
Matthias, Barnabas,

(Ignatius, Alexander,
Marcellinus, Peter,
Felicity, Perpetua,
Agatha, Lucy,
Agnes, Cecilia, Anastasia)
and all your Saints;
admit us, we beseech you,
into their company,
not weighing our merits,
but granting us your pardon,

He joins his hands.

through Christ our Lord.

97. And he continues:

Celebrant alone

Through whom
you continue to make all these good things, O Lord;
you sanctify them, fill them with life,
bless them, and bestow them upon us.

98. He takes the chalice and the paten with the host and, raising both, he says:

Celebrant alone
or with concelebrants

Through him, and with him, and in him,
O God, almighty Father,
in the unity of the Holy Spirit,
all glory and honor is yours,
for ever and ever.

The people acclaim:

Amen.

Then follows the Communion Rite, p. 163.

EUCHARISTIC PRAYER II

99. Although it is provided with its own Preface, this Eucharistic Prayer may also be used with other Prefaces, especially those that present an overall view of the mystery of salvation, such as the Common Prefaces.

℣. **The Lord be with you.**
℟. And with your spirit.

℣. **Lift up your hearts.**
℟. We lift them up to the Lord.

℣. **Let us give thanks to the Lord our God.**
℟. It is right and just.

**It is truly right and just, our duty and our salvation,
always and everywhere to give you thanks, Father most holy,
through your beloved Son, Jesus Christ,
your Word through whom you made all things,
whom you sent as our Savior and Redeemer,
incarnate by the Holy Spirit and born of the Virgin.**

**Fulfilling your will and gaining for you a holy people,
he stretched out his hands as he endured his Passion,
so as to break the bonds of death and manifest the resurrection.**

**And so, with the Angels and all the Saints
we declare your glory,
as with one voice we acclaim:**

**Holy, Holy, Holy Lord God of hosts.
Heaven and earth are full of your glory.
Hosanna in the highest.
Blessed is he who comes in the name of the Lord.
Hosanna in the highest.**

100. The Priest, with hands extended, says:

Celebrant alone

**You are indeed Holy, O Lord,
the fount of all holiness.**

101. He joins his hands and, holding them extended over the offerings, says:

Celebrant alone
or with concelebrants

**Make holy, therefore, these gifts, we pray,
by sending down your Spirit upon them
like the dewfall,**

He joins his hands
and makes the Sign of the Cross once over the bread and the chalice together, saying:

so that they may become for us
the Body and ✠ Blood of our Lord Jesus Christ.

He joins his hands.

102. In the formulas that follow, the words of the Lord should be pronounced clearly and distinctly, as the nature of these words requires.

At the time he was betrayed
and entered willingly into his Passion,

He takes the bread
and, holding it slightly raised above the altar, continues:

he took bread and, giving thanks, broke it,
and gave it to his disciples, saying:

He bows slightly.

TAKE THIS, ALL OF YOU, AND EAT OF IT,
FOR THIS IS MY BODY,
WHICH WILL BE GIVEN UP FOR YOU.

He shows the consecrated host to the people, places it again on the paten, and genuflects in adoration.

103. After this, he continues:

In a similar way, when supper was ended,

He takes the chalice

and, holding it slightly raised above the altar, continues:

he took the chalice
and, once more giving thanks,
he gave it to his disciples, saying:

He bows slightly.

TAKE THIS, ALL OF YOU, AND DRINK FROM IT,
FOR THIS IS THE CHALICE OF MY BLOOD,
THE BLOOD OF THE NEW AND ETERNAL COVENANT,
WHICH WILL BE POURED OUT FOR YOU AND FOR MANY
FOR THE FORGIVENESS OF SINS.

DO THIS IN MEMORY OF ME.

He shows the chalice to the people, places it on the corporal, and genuflects in adoration.

104. Then he says:

Or:

The mystery of faith. Celebrant alone

And the people continue, acclaiming:

We proclaim your Death, O Lord,
and profess your Resurrection
until you come again.

Or:

When we eat this Bread and drink this Cup,
we proclaim your Death, O Lord,
until you come again.

Or:

Save us, Savior of the world,
for by your Cross and Resurrection
you have set us free.

105. Then the Priest, with hands extended, says:

Celebrant with concelebrants

Therefore, as we celebrate
the memorial of his Death and Resurrection,
we offer you, Lord,
the Bread of life and the Chalice of salvation,
giving thanks that you have held us worthy
to be in your presence and minister to you.

Humbly we pray
that, partaking of the Body and Blood of Christ,
we may be gathered into one by the Holy Spirit.

Celebrant or one concelebrant

Remember, Lord, your Church,
spread throughout the world,
and bring her to the fullness of charity,
together with N. our Pope and N. our Bishop*[*]
and all the clergy.

In Masses for the Dead, the following may be added:

Remember your servant N.,
whom you have called (today)
from this world to yourself.
Grant that he (she) who was united with your Son in a death like his,
may also be one with him in his Resurrection.

---

* Mention may be made here of the Coadjutor Bishop, or Auxiliary Bishops, as noted in the *General Instruction of the Roman Missal*, no. 149.

Celebrant or one concelebrant

Remember also our brothers and sisters
who have fallen asleep in the hope of
the resurrection,
and all who have died in your mercy:
welcome them into the light of your face.
Have mercy on us all, we pray,
that with the Blessed Virgin Mary, Mother of God,
with the blessed Apostles,
and all the Saints who have pleased you throughout the ages,
we may merit to be coheirs to eternal life,
and may praise and glorify you

He joins his hands.

through your Son, Jesus Christ.

106. He takes the chalice and the paten with the host and, raising both, he says:

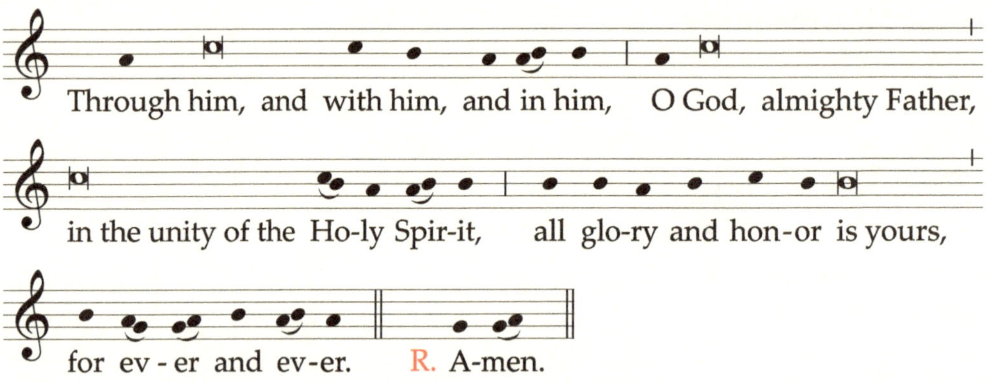

Celebrant with concelebrants

Through him, and with him, and in him,
O God, almighty Father,
in the unity of the Holy Spirit,
all glory and honor is yours,
for ever and ever.

The people acclaim:

Amen.

Then follows the Communion Rite, p. 163.

EUCHARISTIC PRAYER III

107. ℣. **The Lord be with you.**
℟. And with your spirit.

℣. **Lift up your hearts.**
℟. We lift them up to the Lord.

℣. **Let us give thanks to the Lord our God.**
℟. It is right and just.

Then follows the Preface to be used in accord with the rubrics, which concludes:

Holy, Holy, Holy Lord God of hosts.
Heaven and earth are full of your glory.
Hosanna in the highest.
Blessed is he who comes in the name of the Lord.
Hosanna in the highest.

108. *The Priest, with hands extended, says:*

Celebrant alone

You are indeed Holy, O Lord,
and all you have created
rightly gives you praise,
for through your Son our Lord Jesus Christ,
by the power and working of the Holy Spirit,
you give life to all things and make them holy,
and you never cease to gather a people to yourself,
so that from the rising of the sun to its setting
a pure sacrifice may be offered to your name.

109. *He joins his hands and, holding them extended over the offerings, says:*

Celebrant with concelebrants

Therefore, O Lord, we humbly implore you:
by the same Spirit graciously make holy
these gifts we have brought to you for consecration,

He joins his hands
and makes the Sign of the Cross once over the bread and chalice together, saying:

that they may become the Body and ✠ Blood
of your Son our Lord Jesus Christ,

He joins his hands.

at whose command we celebrate these mysteries.

110. In the formulas that follow, the words of the Lord should be pronounced clearly and distinctly, as the nature of these words requires.

For on the night he was betrayed

He takes the bread

and, holding it slightly raised above the altar, continues:

he himself took bread,
and, giving you thanks, he said the blessing,
broke the bread and gave it to his disciples, saying:

He bows slightly.

TAKE THIS, ALL OF YOU, AND EAT OF IT,
FOR THIS IS MY BODY,
WHICH WILL BE GIVEN UP FOR YOU.

He shows the consecrated host to the people, places it again on the paten, and genuflects in adoration.

111. After this, he continues:

In a similar way, when supper was ended,

He takes the chalice
and, holding it slightly raised above the altar, continues:

he took the chalice,
and, giving you thanks, he said the blessing,
and gave the chalice to his disciples, saying:

He bows slightly.

TAKE THIS, ALL OF YOU, AND DRINK FROM IT,
FOR THIS IS THE CHALICE OF MY BLOOD,
THE BLOOD OF THE NEW AND ETERNAL COVENANT,
WHICH WILL BE POURED OUT FOR YOU AND FOR MANY
FOR THE FORGIVENESS OF SINS.

DO THIS IN MEMORY OF ME.

He shows the chalice to the people, places it on the corporal, and genuflects in adoration.

112. Then he says:

Or:

The mystery of faith. Celebrant alone

And the people continue, acclaiming:

We proclaim your Death, O Lord,
and profess your Resurrection
until you come again.

Or:

When we eat this Bread and drink this Cup,
we proclaim your Death, O Lord,
until you come again.

Or:

Save us, Savior of the world,
for by your Cross and Resurrection
you have set us free.

113. Then the Priest, with hands extended, says:

Celebrant with concelebrants

**Therefore, O Lord, as we celebrate the memorial
of the saving Passion of your Son,
his wondrous Resurrection
and Ascension into heaven,
and as we look forward to his second coming,
we offer you in thanksgiving
this holy and living sacrifice.**

**Look, we pray, upon the oblation of your Church
and, recognizing the sacrificial Victim by whose death
you willed to reconcile us to yourself,
grant that we, who are nourished
by the Body and Blood of your Son
and filled with his Holy Spirit,
may become one body, one spirit in Christ.**

Celebrant or one concelebrant

**May he make of us
an eternal offering to you,
so that we may obtain an inheritance with your elect,
especially with the most Blessed Virgin Mary, Mother of God,
with your blessed Apostles and glorious Martyrs
(with Saint N.: the Saint of the day or Patron Saint)
and with all the Saints,
on whose constant intercession in your presence
we rely for unfailing help.**

Celebrant or one concelebrant

**May this Sacrifice of our reconciliation,
we pray, O Lord,
advance the peace and salvation of all the world.
Be pleased to confirm in faith and charity
your pilgrim Church on earth,
with your servant N. our Pope and N. our Bishop,***
**the Order of Bishops, all the clergy,
and the entire people you have gained for your own.**

* Mention may be made here of the Coadjutor Bishop, or Auxiliary Bishops, as noted in the *General Instruction of the Roman Missal*, no. 149.

Listen graciously to the prayers of this family,
whom you have summoned before you:
in your compassion, O merciful Father,
gather to yourself all your children
scattered throughout the world.

† **To our departed brothers and sisters**
and to all who were pleasing to you
at their passing from this life,
give kind admittance to your kingdom.
There we hope to enjoy for ever the fullness of your glory

Celebrant or one concelebrant

He joins his hands.

through Christ our Lord,
through whom you bestow on the world all that is good. †

114. He takes the chalice and the paten with the host and, raising both, he says:

Through him, and with him, and in him,
O God, almighty Father,
in the unity of the Holy Spirit,
all glory and honor is yours,
for ever and ever.

Celebrant alone or with concelebrants

The people acclaim:

Amen.

Then follows the Communion Rite, p. 163.

115. When this Eucharistic Prayer is used in Masses for the Dead, the following may be said:

† Remember your servant N.
whom you have called (today)
from this world to yourself.
Grant that he (she) who was united with your Son in a death like his,
may also be one with him in his Resurrection,
when from the earth
he will raise up in the flesh those who have died,
and transform our lowly body
after the pattern of his own glorious body.
To our departed brothers and sisters, too,
and to all who were pleasing to you
at their passing from this life,
give kind admittance to your kingdom.
There we hope to enjoy for ever the fullness of your glory,
when you will wipe away every tear from our eyes.
For seeing you, our God, as you are,
we shall be like you for all the ages
and praise you without end,

He joins his hands.

through Christ our Lord,
through whom you bestow on the world all that is good. †

EUCHARISTIC PRAYER IV

116. It is not permitted to change the Preface of this Eucharistic Prayer because of the structure of the Prayer itself, which presents a summary of the history of salvation.

℣. **The Lord be with you.**
℟. And with your spirit.

℣. **Lift up your hearts.**
℟. We lift them up to the Lord.

℣. **Let us give thanks to the Lord our God.**
℟. It is right and just.

It is truly right to give you thanks,
truly just to give you glory, Father most holy,
for you are the one God living and true,
existing before all ages and abiding for all eternity,
dwelling in unapproachable light;
yet you, who alone are good, the source of life,
have made all that is,
so that you might fill your creatures with blessings
and bring joy to many of them by the glory of your light.

And so, in your presence are countless hosts of Angels,
who serve you day and night
and, gazing upon the glory of your face,
glorify you without ceasing.

With them we, too, confess your name in exultation,
giving voice to every creature under heaven,
as we acclaim:

Holy, Holy, Holy Lord God of hosts.
Heaven and earth are full of your glory.
Hosanna in the highest.
Blessed is he who comes in the name of the Lord.
Hosanna in the highest.

117. The Priest, with hands extended, says:

Celebrant alone

We give you praise, Father most holy,
for you are great
and you have fashioned all your works
in wisdom and in love.
You formed man in your own image
and entrusted the whole world to his care,
so that in serving you alone, the Creator,
he might have dominion over all creatures.
And when through disobedience he had lost your friendship,
you did not abandon him to the domain of death.
For you came in mercy to the aid of all,
so that those who seek might find you.
Time and again you offered them covenants
and through the prophets
taught them to look forward to salvation.

And you so loved the world, Father most holy,
that in the fullness of time
you sent your Only Begotten Son to be our Savior.
Made incarnate by the Holy Spirit
and born of the Virgin Mary,
he shared our human nature
in all things but sin.
To the poor he proclaimed the good news of salvation,
to prisoners, freedom,
and to the sorrowful of heart, joy.
To accomplish your plan,
he gave himself up to death,
and, rising from the dead,
he destroyed death and restored life.

And that we might live no longer for ourselves
but for him who died and rose again for us,
he sent the Holy Spirit from you, Father,
as the first fruits for those who believe,
so that, bringing to perfection his work in the world,
he might sanctify creation to the full.

118. *He joins his hands and, holding them extended over the offerings, says:*

Celebrant with concelebrants

Therefore, O Lord, we pray:
may this same Holy Spirit
graciously sanctify these offerings,

He joins his hands and makes the Sign of the Cross once over the bread and chalice together, saying:

that they may become
the Body and ✠ Blood of our Lord Jesus Christ

He joins his hands.

for the celebration of this great mystery,
which he himself left us
as an eternal covenant.

119. *In the formulas that follow, the words of the Lord should be pronounced clearly and distinctly, as the nature of these words requires.*

For when the hour had come
for him to be glorified by you, Father most holy,
having loved his own who were in the world,
he loved them to the end:
and while they were at supper,

He takes the bread and, holding it slightly raised above the altar, continues:

he took bread, blessed and broke it,
and gave it to his disciples, saying:

He bows slightly.

TAKE THIS, ALL OF YOU, AND EAT OF IT,
FOR THIS IS MY BODY,
WHICH WILL BE GIVEN UP FOR YOU.

He shows the consecrated host to the people, places it again on the paten, and genuflects in adoration.

120. *After this, he continues:*

In a similar way,

He takes the chalice and, holding it slightly raised above the altar, continues:

taking the chalice filled with the fruit of the vine,
he gave thanks,
and gave the chalice to his disciples, saying:

He bows slightly.

TAKE THIS, ALL OF YOU, AND DRINK FROM IT,
FOR THIS IS THE CHALICE OF MY BLOOD,
THE BLOOD OF THE NEW AND ETERNAL COVENANT,
WHICH WILL BE POURED OUT FOR YOU AND FOR MANY
FOR THE FORGIVENESS OF SINS.
DO THIS IN MEMORY OF ME.

He shows the chalice to the people, places it on the corporal, and genuflects in adoration.

121. Then he says:

Or:

The mystery of faith. Celebrant alone

And the people continue, acclaiming:

We proclaim your Death, O Lord,
and profess your Resurrection
until you come again.

Or:

When we eat this Bread and drink this Cup,
we proclaim your Death, O Lord,
until you come again.

Or:

Save us, Savior of the world,
for by your Cross and Resurrection
you have set us free.

122. Then, with hands extended, the Priest says:

Celebrant with concelebrants

**Therefore, O Lord,
as we now celebrate the memorial of our redemption,
we remember Christ's Death
and his descent to the realm of the dead,
we proclaim his Resurrection
and his Ascension to your right hand,
and, as we await his coming in glory,
we offer you his Body and Blood,
the sacrifice acceptable to you
which brings salvation to the whole world.**

**Look, O Lord, upon the Sacrifice
which you yourself have provided for your Church,
and grant in your loving kindness
to all who partake of this one Bread and one Chalice
that, gathered into one body by the Holy Spirit,
they may truly become a living sacrifice in Christ
to the praise of your glory.**

Celebrant or one concelebrant

**Therefore, Lord, remember now
all for whom we offer this sacrifice:
especially your servant** N. **our Pope,**
N. **our Bishop,*** **and the whole Order of Bishops,
all the clergy,**

* Mention may be made here of the Coadjutor Bishop, or Auxiliary Bishops, as noted in the *General Instruction of the Roman Missal*, no. 149.

those who take part in this offering,
those gathered here before you,
your entire people,
and all who seek you with a sincere heart.

Remember also
those who have died in the peace of your Christ
and all the dead,
whose faith you alone have known.

Celebrant or one concelebrant

To all of us, your children,
grant, O merciful Father,
that we may enter into a heavenly inheritance
with the Blessed Virgin Mary, Mother of God,
and with your Apostles and Saints in your kingdom.
There, with the whole of creation,
freed from the corruption of sin and death,
may we glorify you through Christ our Lord,

He joins his hands.

through whom you bestow on the world all that is good.

123. He takes the chalice and the paten with the host and, raising both, he says:

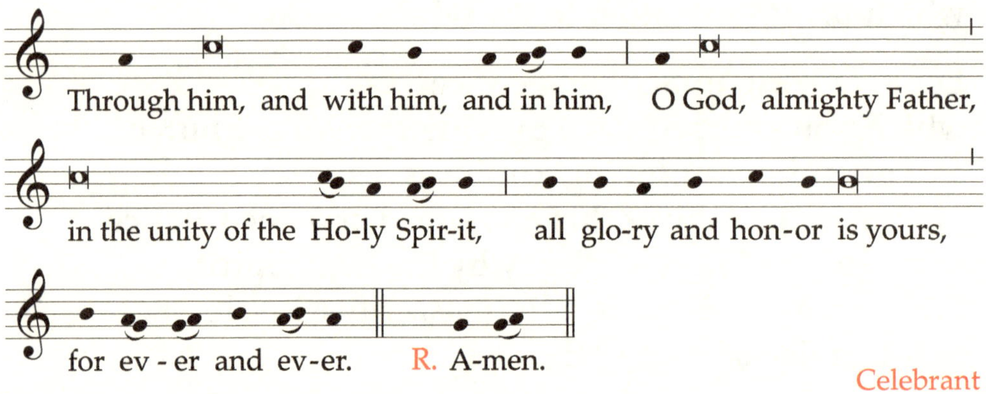

Celebrant alone or with concelebrants

Through him, and with him, and in him,
O God, almighty Father,
in the unity of the Holy Spirit,
all glory and honor is yours,
for ever and ever.

The people acclaim:

Amen.

Then follows the Communion Rite, p. 163.

The Communion Rite

124. After the chalice and paten have been set down, the Priest, with hands joined, says:

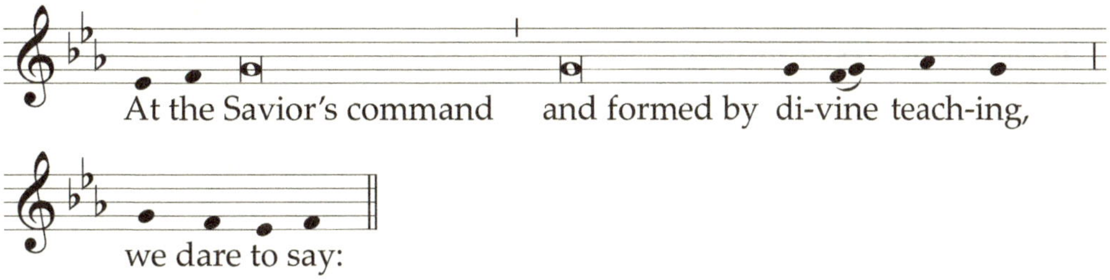

**At the Savior's command
and formed by divine teaching,
we dare to say:**

He extends his hands and, together with the people, continues:

**Our Father, who art in heaven,
hallowed be thy name;
thy kingdom come,
thy will be done
on earth as it is in heaven.**

Give us this day our daily bread,
and forgive us our trespasses,
as we forgive those who trespass against us;
and lead us not into temptation,
but deliver us from evil.

Or:

125. With hands extended, the Priest alone continues, saying:

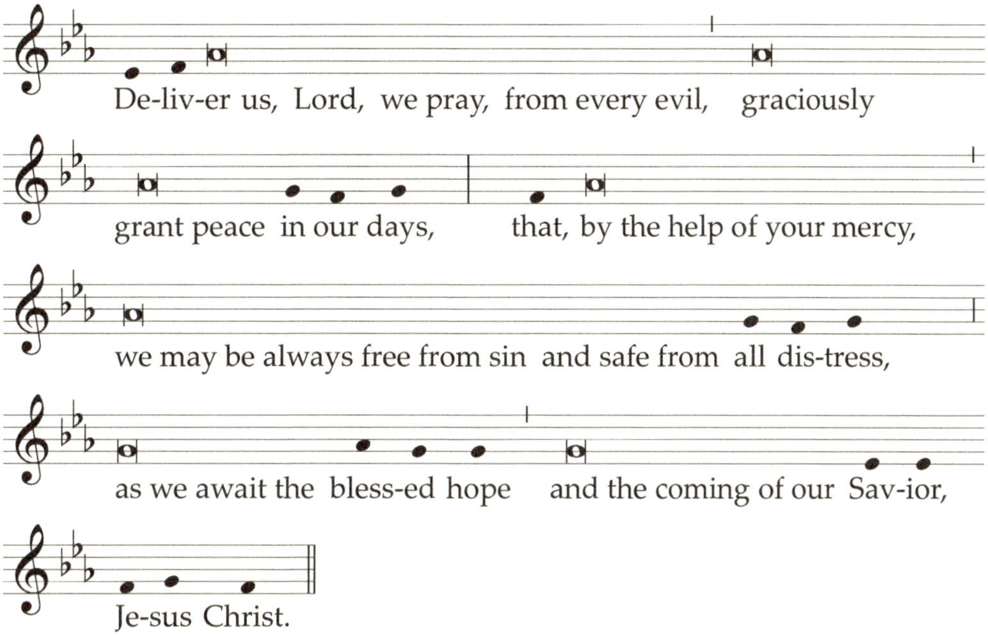

Deliver us, Lord, we pray, from every evil,
graciously grant peace in our days,
that, by the help of your mercy,
we may be always free from sin
and safe from all distress,
as we await the blessed hope
and the coming of our Savior, Jesus Christ.

He joins his hands.

The people conclude the prayer, acclaiming:

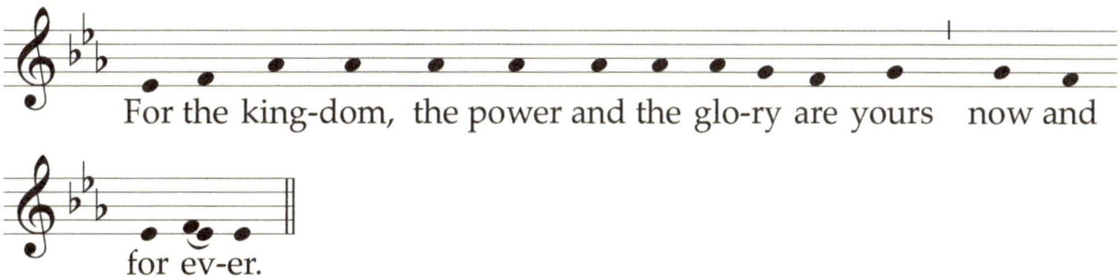

For the kingdom,
the power and the glory are yours
now and for ever.

126. Then the Priest, with hands extended, says aloud:

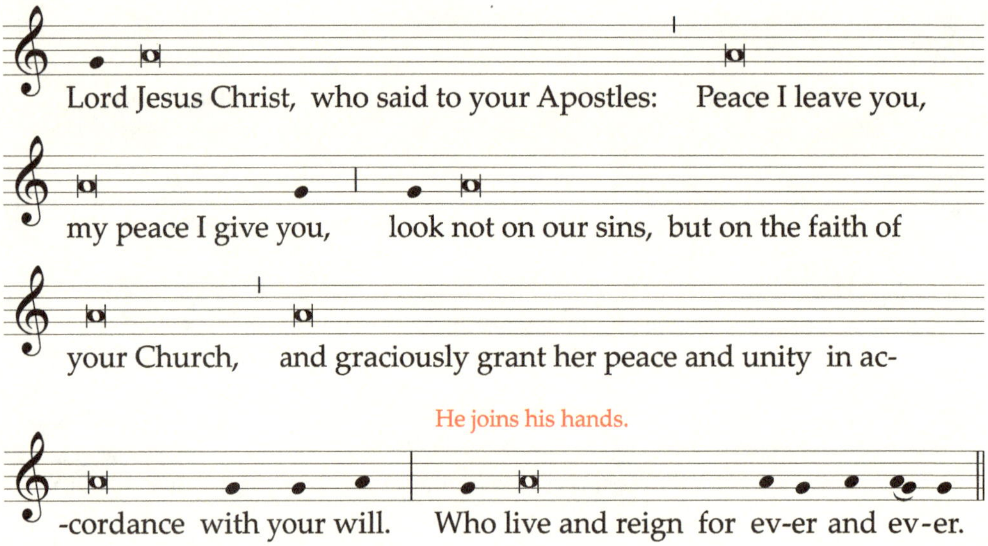

Lord Jesus Christ,
who said to your Apostles:
Peace I leave you, my peace I give you,
look not on our sins,
but on the faith of your Church,
and graciously grant her peace and unity
in accordance with your will.

He joins his hands.

Who live and reign for ever and ever.

The people reply:

Amen.

127. The Priest, turned towards the people, extending and then joining his hands, adds:

The peace of the Lord be with you always.

The people reply:

And with your spirit.

128. Then, if appropriate, the Deacon, or the Priest, adds:

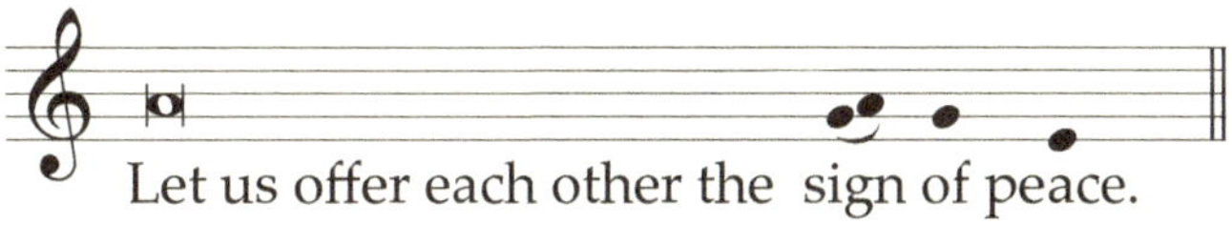

Let us offer each other the sign of peace.

And all offer one another a sign, in keeping with local customs, that expresses peace, communion, and charity. The Priest gives the sign of peace to a Deacon or minister.

129. Then he takes the host, breaks it over the paten, and places a small piece in the chalice, saying quietly:

May this mingling of the Body and Blood
of our Lord Jesus Christ
bring eternal life to us who receive it.

130. Meanwhile the following is sung or said:

Lamb of God, you take away the sins of the world,
have mercy on us.
Lamb of God, you take away the sins of the world,
have mercy on us.
Lamb of God, you take away the sins of the world,
grant us peace.

Or:

The invocation may even be repeated several times if the fraction is prolonged. Only the final time, however, is grant us peace said.

131. Then the Priest, with hands joined, says quietly:

Lord Jesus Christ, Son of the living God,
who, by the will of the Father
and the work of the Holy Spirit,
through your Death gave life to the world,
free me by this, your most holy Body and Blood,
from all my sins and from every evil;
keep me always faithful to your commandments,
and never let me be parted from you.

Or:

May the receiving of your Body and Blood,
Lord Jesus Christ,
not bring me to judgment and condemnation,
but through your loving mercy
be for me protection in mind and body
and a healing remedy.

132. The Priest genuflects, takes the host and, holding it slightly raised above the paten or above the chalice, while facing the people, says aloud:

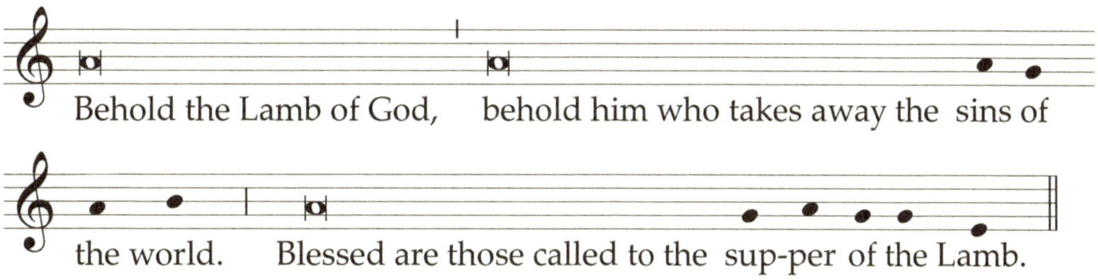

Behold the Lamb of God,
behold him who takes away the sins of the world.
Blessed are those called to the supper of the Lamb.

And together with the people he adds once:

Lord, I am not worthy
that you should enter under my roof,
but only say the word
and my soul shall be healed.

133. The Priest, facing the altar, says quietly:

May the Body of Christ
keep me safe for eternal life.

And he reverently consumes the Body of Christ.

Then he takes the chalice and says quietly:

May the Blood of Christ
keep me safe for eternal life.

And he reverently consumes the Blood of Christ.

134. After this, he takes the paten or ciborium and approaches the communicants. The Priest raises a host slightly and shows it to each of the communicants, saying:

The Body of Christ.

The communicant replies:

Amen.

And receives Holy Communion.

If a Deacon also distributes Holy Communion, he does so in the same manner.

135. If any are present who are to receive Holy Communion under both kinds, the rite described in the proper place is to be followed.

136. While the Priest is receiving the Body of Christ, the Communion Chant begins.

137. When the distribution of Communion is over, the Priest or a Deacon or an acolyte purifies the paten over the chalice and also the chalice itself.

While he carries out the purification, the Priest says quietly:

What has passed our lips as food, O Lord,
may we possess in purity of heart,
that what has been given to us in time
may be our healing for eternity.

138. Then the Priest may return to the chair. If appropriate, a sacred silence may be observed for a while, or a psalm or other canticle of praise or a hymn may be sung.

139. Then, standing at the altar or at the chair and facing the people, with hands joined, the Priest says:

Let us pray.

All pray in silence with the Priest for a while, unless silence has just been observed. Then the Priest, with hands extended, says the Prayer after Communion, at the end of which the people acclaim:

Amen.

The Concluding Rites

140. If they are necessary, any brief announcements to the people follow here.

141. Then the dismissal takes place. The Priest, facing the people and extending his hands, says:

The Lord be with you.

The people reply:

And with your spirit.

The Priest blesses the people, saying:

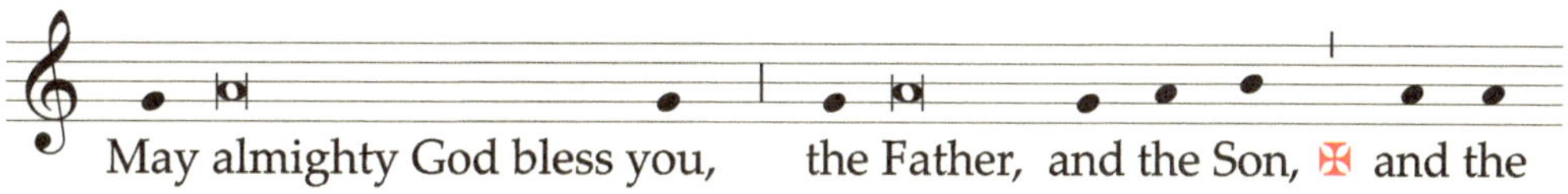

May almighty God bless you,
the Father, and the Son, ✠ and the Holy Spirit.

The people reply:

Amen.

---

142. On certain days or occasions, this formula of blessing is preceded, in accordance with the rubrics, by another more solemn formula of blessing (cf. pp. 175ff.).

---

143. In a Pontifical Mass, the celebrant receives the miter and, extending his hands, says:

The Lord be with you.

All reply:

And with your spirit.

The celebrant says:

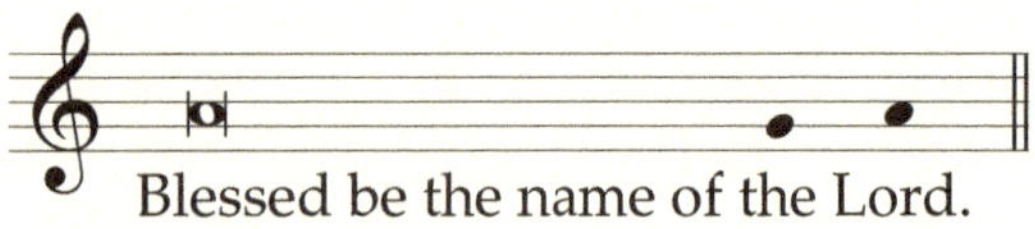

Blessed be the name of the Lord.

All reply:

Now and for ever.

The celebrant says:

Our help is in the name of the Lord.

All reply:

Who made heaven and earth.

Then the celebrant receives the pastoral staff, if he uses it, and says:

May almighty God bless you,

making the Sign of the Cross over the people three times, he adds:

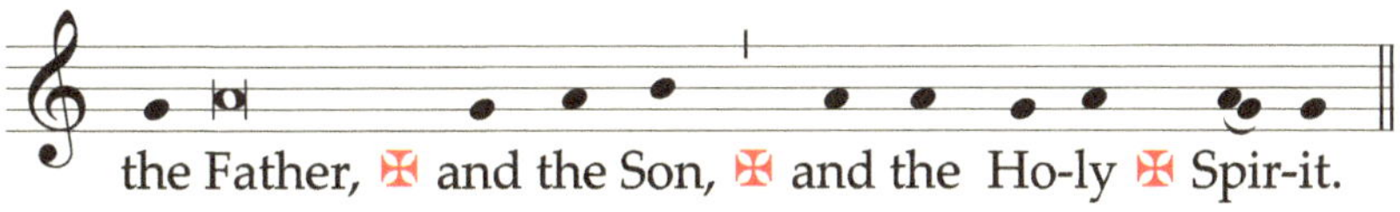

the Father, ✠ and the Son, ✠ and the Holy ✠ Spirit.

All:

Amen.

---

144. Then the Deacon, or the Priest himself, with hands joined and facing the people, says:

Go forth, the Mass is ended.

Or:

Go and announce the Gospel of the Lord.

Or:

Go in peace, glorifying the Lord by your life.

Or:

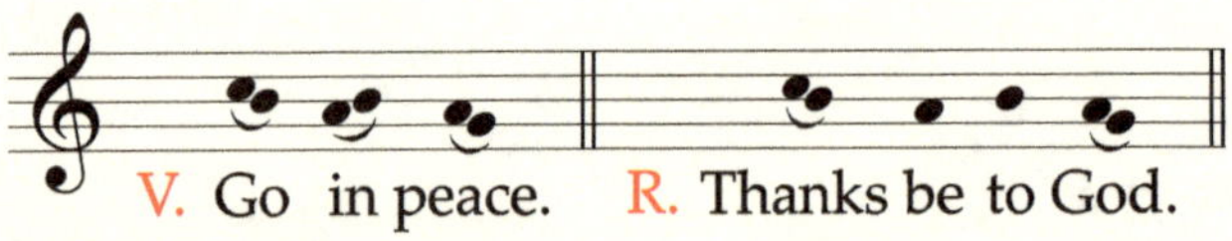

Go in peace.

The people reply:

Thanks be to God.

145. Then the Priest venerates the altar as usual with a kiss, as at the beginning. After making a profound bow with the ministers, he withdraws.

146. If any liturgical action follows immediately, the rites of dismissal are omitted.

SOLEMN BLESSINGS

The following blessings may be used, at the discretion of the Priest, at the end of the celebration of Mass, or of a Liturgy of the Word, or of the Office, or of the Sacraments.

The Deacon or, in his absence, the Priest himself, says the invitation: Bow down for the blessing. Then the Priest, with hands extended over the people, says the blessing, with all responding: Amen.

ADVENT

May you be filled with the grace of God the Father,
whose Word was conceived in the womb of the Blessed Virgin
to become the Savior of the human race.
℟. Amen.

May your hearts never lose the peace of Christ,
whose coming the Blessed Virgin, daughter of Zion,
so joyously awaited.
℟. Amen.

May the light and grace of the Holy Spirit remain with you,
that you may await the Second Coming of Christ
vigilant in prayer and with songs of praise on your lips.
℟. Amen.

And may the blessing of almighty God,
the Father, and the Son, ✠ and the Holy Spirit,
come down on you and remain with you for ever.
℟. Amen.

CHRISTMAS TIME

May God, who through the motherhood of the Virgin Mary
dispelled the darkness of ages past,
enlighten your minds with the radiance of the sun of justice.
℟. Amen.

May God, who sent his Son as the Redeemer of the world,
refashion your minds and hearts in the image of Christ.
℟. Amen.

Like Mary, Mother of Wisdom,
may you gratefully ponder in your hearts
the wonder of God's blessings
and may you find in Christ and the Blessed Virgin
the model of your way of life.
℟. Amen.

And may the blessing of almighty God,
the Father, and the Son, ✠ and the Holy Spirit,
come down on you and remain with you for ever.
℟. Amen.

LENT

Through the sacrifice of Christ,
to which his sorrowful Mother united her own loving heart,
God chose to redeem the human race.
May he draw you deeply into that great mystery of salvation.
℟. Amen.

God led the Blessed Virgin Mary to advance even further
in faith and in sorrow
until at the foot of the Cross she reached the perfection of charity.
May he make your faith ever stronger
and inspire you to love him
with your whole heart and soul and strength.
℟. Amen.

And when the days of your life are ended,
may you reflect the image of Christ in his Passion,
that you may become sharers in his glory.
℟. Amen.

And may the blessing of almighty God,
the Father, and the Son, ✠ and the Holy Spirit,
come down on you and remain with you for ever.
℟. Amen.

EASTER TIME

**God the Father, through the Resurrection of his Son,
gladdened the Blessed Virgin and the infant Church;
may he fill you with every spiritual joy and peace.**
℟. Amen.

**Jesus Christ, who was born of a spotless Virgin,
arose incorruptible from the grave;
may he preserve undiminished in your hearts
the fullness of your baptismal faith.**
℟. Amen.

**May the Holy Spirit,
whose coming the Blessed Virgin, with the Apostles,
awaited in sure faith,
dwell with you to purify your hearts.**
℟. Amen.

**And may the blessing of almighty God,
the Father, and the Son, ✠ and the Holy Spirit,
come down on you and remain with you for ever.**
℟. Amen.

ORDINARY TIME
I

**May the Father of all mercy,
through the love with which he cherished the Mother of his Son,
bless you with health of mind and body.**
℟. Amen.

**May Jesus Christ, the blessed fruit of Mary's womb,
adorn you with the virtues
that will make you more pleasing to him.**
℟. Amen.

May the Holy Spirit,
whose power overshadowed the Blessed Virgin,
give you serenity and peace,
that you may live as one in mind and heart
in the household of the Church.
℟. Amen.

And may the blessing of almighty God,
the Father, and the Son, ✠ and the Holy Spirit,
come down on you and remain with you for ever.
℟. Amen.

II

May God, who through the childbearing of the Blessed Virgin Mary
willed in his great kindness to redeem the human race,
be pleased to enrich you with his blessing.
℟. Amen.

May you know always and everywhere the protection of her,
through whom you have been found worthy to receive the author of life.
℟. Amen.
May you, who have devoutly gathered to celebrate this memorial of our Lady,
carry away with you the gifts of spiritual joys and heavenly rewards.
℟. Amen.

And may the blessing of almighty God,
the Father, and the Son, ✠ and the Holy Spirit,
come down on you and remain with you for ever.
℟. Amen.

III

May the Father of mercies bless you
through the intercession of Blessed Mary ever-Virgin
through whom he chose to remedy the fall of our first parents.
℟. Amen.

May Jesus Christ, who in the womb of the Blessed Virgin
became our brother and our Savior,
free your hearts from every trace of sin.
℟. Amen.

May the Holy Spirit
increase in you the grace of true faith and of hope for heaven,
that you may walk in the ways of the Gospel
and so reach your eternal home.
℟. Amen.

And may the blessing of almighty God,
the Father, and the Son, ✠ and the Holy Spirit,
come down on you and remain with you for ever.
℟. Amen.

ORDINARY TIME

During Ordinary Time memorials of the Blessed Virgin occur frequently both in the General Roman Calendar and in the calendars of the particular Churches and of religious institutes. There are consequently a great number of Marian Mass formularies in propers of the Roman Rite, which have one and the same object—the work God has accomplished in Mary in relationship to Christ and the Church—but which celebrate it under its many different aspects.

In view of the mystery that they celebrate the Mass formularies for Ordinary Time are divided into three sections. The first section contains eleven formularies to celebrate memorials of the Mother of God under titles that are derived chiefly from Sacred Scripture or that express Mary's bond with the Church. The second section contains nine formularies to celebrate memorials of the Blessed Virgin Mary under titles that refer to her cooperation in fostering the spiritual life of the faithful. The third section contains eight formularies to celebrate memorials of the Blessed Virgin under titles that suggest her compassionate intercession on behalf of the faithful (cf. *Collection of Masses of the Blessed Virgin Mary*, Introduction, no. 24).

SECTION 1

This section contains eleven Mass formularies for the celebration of a memorial of the Mother of God under titles that are chiefly derived from Scripture or that bring out Mary's bond with the Church.

MASS FORMULARIES

19. Holy Mary, Mother of the Lord
20. Holy Mary, the New Eve
21. The Holy Name of the Blessed Virgin Mary
22. Holy Mary, Handmaid of the Lord
23. The Blessed Virgin Mary, Temple of the Lord
24. The Blessed Virgin Mary, Seat of Wisdom
25. The Blessed Virgin Mary, Image and Mother of the Church, I
26. The Blessed Virgin Mary, Image and Mother of the Church, II
27. The Blessed Virgin Mary, Image and Mother of the Church, III
28. The Immaculate Heart of the Blessed Virgin Mary
29. The Blessed Virgin Mary, Queen of All Creation

19. HOLY MARY, MOTHER OF THE LORD

Among the titles given to the Blessed Virgin in the Gospels that of "Mother of the Lord" has a special place. Elizabeth, the mother of Christ's herald, filled with the Holy Spirit (cf. Luke 1:41), used this title in greeting our Lady: "How does this happen to me, that the Mother of my Lord should come to me?" (Luke 1:43).

Under the title of "Holy Mary, Mother of the Lord," the formulary provided here, with the exception of the Prayer after Communion and the Preface, is the Mass found in *The Roman Missal*, Common of the Blessed Virgin Mary, Ordinary Time, no. 3, the texts of which are marked by what is known as "Roman sobriety" and by deep devotion to the Mother of Jesus. The Preface is taken from the *Proprium missarum Societatis Apostolatus Catholici*, Curia Generalis Ordinis, Rome, 1976, p. 11.

In the Preface God the Father is glorified on account of the double maternal role he has assigned in his "wisdom and love" to the Blessed Virgin: in relation to his Son ("In the Mother of your Son you showed the wonders of your power") and in relation to his people ("she fulfills a mother's role in the household of the Church").

Entrance Antiphon Cf. Judith 13:18-19

Blessed are you, O Virgin Mary, by the Lord God Most High,
above all women on the earth;
for he has so exalted your name
that your praise shall be undying on our lips.

COLLECT

As we venerate the glorious memory
of the most holy Virgin Mary, Mother of the Lord,
grant, we pray, O Lord, through her intercession,
that we, too, may merit to receive
from the fullness of your grace.
Through our Lord Jesus Christ, your Son,
who lives and reigns with you in the unity of the Holy Spirit,
God, for ever and ever.

PRAYER OVER THE OFFERINGS

We offer you the sacrifice of praise, O Lord,
as we rejoice in commemorating the Mother of your Son,
grant, we pray,
that through this most holy exchange
we may advance towards eternal redemption.
Through Christ our Lord.

Preface P 19, page 103.

Communion Antiphon Cf. Luke 1:48

All generations will call me blessed,
for God has looked on his lowly handmaid.

PRAYER AFTER COMMUNION

Having received this heavenly Sacrament,
we humbly pray, O Lord
that we, who reverently celebrate the Memorial of the Blessed Virgin Mary,
may merit to be partakers at your eternal banquet.
Through Christ our Lord.

20. HOLY MARY, THE NEW EVE

As early as the second century, especially in the writings of St. Justin (d. c. 163) and St. Irenaeus (d. c. 200), the Blessed Virgin Mary is seen by the Church as the new Eve or the new woman, intimately associated with Christ, the new Adam (cf. 1 Corinthians 15:45), in the work of salvation. By her faith and obedience she undoes the loss inflicted on the human race by the unbelief and disobedience of the first Eve: "The knot of Eve's disobedience was loosed by Mary's obedience. The bonds fastened by the virgin Eve through disbelief were untied by the virgin Mary through faith" (St. Irenaeus, *Adversus haereses,* 3:22, 4: Sch, no. 34, p. 82).

In this formulary the saving "mystery of the woman"—of Mary and the Church—is commemorated. Mary, as "type of the Church" (cf. LG, no. 63), is the woman promised in the Proto-Gospel (cf. Genesis 3:15), greeted by Elizabeth as blessed among all women (cf. Luke 1:42), from whom the Son of God became truly human (cf. Galatians 4:4), anticipating the mysterious "hour" of Jesus at the wedding feast at Cana (cf. John 2:4), fulfilling her role of mother at the foot of the Cross (cf. John 19:26), resplendent in heaven as the woman clothed with the sun and crowned with stars (cf. Revelation 12:1).

Mary is thus celebrated as:

—*the firstfruits of the new creation:* "you chose the Blessed Virgin, formed by the Holy Spirit, as the firstfruits of the new creation" (Col; cf. LG, no. 56).

—*the new earth,* where, from the moment of her Immaculate Conception, "justice dwells" (cf. Resp).

—*the firstfruits of the new people of God:* "you made her the firstfruits of your new people" (Pref).

—*a disciple of the New Law:* "the first disciple of the New Law" (Pref).

—*a woman given a new heart by God,* in accordance with the prophecy of Ezekiel (cf. 1:9): "you formed a new heart for the second Eve" (PC).

—*a woman preparing the new wine for the Church:* "blessed are you, Virgin Mary . . . through you Christ has prepared the new wine for the Church" (Com Ant, B).

—*a faithful virgin:* "we celebrate the memory of the Blessed Virgin Mary and her complete self-giving to the sacrifice of the New Law" (PO).

—*the new Jerusalem,* the holy city, the dwelling-place of God (cf. 1 Read, Revelation 21:1-5a).

To sum up: Holy Mary, "conceived without stain, enriched by gifts of grace, . . . is indeed the new woman" (Pref), Mother and companion of Christ, author of the New Covenant (cf. Pref).

Entrance Antiphon Revelation 12:1

A great sign appeared in heaven:
a woman clothed with the sun, the moon beneath her feet,
and on her head a crown of twelve stars.

COLLECT

Lord our God, you chose the Blessed Virgin,
formed by the Holy Spirit,
as the firstfruits of the new creation;
grant that we may reject the old ways of sin,
embrace wholeheartedly the new life of the Gospel,
and honor faithfully the new commandment of love.
Through our Lord Jesus Christ, your Son,
who lives and reigns with you in the unity of the Holy Spirit,
God, for ever and ever.

PRAYER OVER THE OFFERINGS

Lord,
as we celebrate the memory of the Blessed Virgin Mary
and her complete self-giving
to the sacrifice of the New Law,
we offer you these gifts
as a sign of our worship
and ask that by the power of your grace
we may walk all our days
in the new life you have given us.
Through Christ our Lord.

Preface P 20, page 104.

Communion Antiphon

A **Glorious things are spoken of you, O Virgin Mary,** Cf. Psalm 87:3; Luke 1:49
for he who is mighty has done great things for you.

B **Blessed are you, Virgin Mary:**
through you God has given us the Savior of the world,
through you Christ has prepared the new wine for the Church.

PRAYER AFTER COMMUNION

Lord our God,
in the Blessed Virgin Mary
you formed a new heart for the second Eve;
grant that by the grace of this Sacrament
we may be obedient to the inspiration of the Holy Spirit
and grow more and more each day
in the likeness of Christ, the second Adam.
Who lives and reigns for ever and ever.

21. THE HOLY NAME OF THE BLESSED VIRGIN MARY

The Roman Missal has a Votive Mass of the Most Holy Name of Mary, of which only the opening prayer is proper. A memorial of the Most Holy Name of the Virgin is celebrated on 12 September in many particular Churches and religious institutes, generally with the same formulary. The present formulary, except for the Preface and a few changes, is taken from the *Proprium missarum Societatis Mariae*.

In this Mass God the Father is glorified first of all on account of "the name of Jesus," that is, on account of "the person of his Son," his power and saving mission: "In no other name is there salvation" (Pref, cf. Acts 4:12); "at his command every knee must bend, in heaven, on earth, and under the earth" (Pref, cf. Philippians 2:10).

The Father is then glorified on account of "the name of Mary," that is, on account of the person of Christ's Mother and her mission in the history of salvation (cf. Pref). The name of the Blessed Virgin Mary is celebrated as:

—*a name of honor*, for God "has so exalted your Name that your praise shall be undying on our lips," as he brought honor to the name of Judith, who is a type of the Blessed Virgin (Ent Ant, cf. Judith 13:20);

—*a holy name*, for it marks out the woman who was entirely "full of grace" (*All*, cf. Luke 1:28) and found "favor with God" (Gos, Luke 1:30) and so conceived and gave birth to the Son of God (cf. Luke 1:31);

—*a maternal name*, for the Lord Jesus, "dying on the altar of the Cross, willed that the most Blessed Virgin Mary, whom he had chosen as his Mother, should be our mother also," (Col), so that the faithful as they "fly to her protection, may find comfort" (Col);

—*a name responsive to need*, for the faithful on whose lips the name of the Virgin echoes and re-echoes (cf. Pref) "turn to her with confidence as their star of hope, call on her as their mother in time of danger, and seek her protection in their hour of need" (Pref, cf. Col).

Entrance Antiphon Cf. Judith 13:18-19

Blessed are you, O Virgin Mary, by the Lord God Most High,
above all women on the earth;
for he has so exalted your Name
that your praise shall be undying on our lips.

COLLECT

O God, whose Son, dying on the altar of the Cross,
willed that the most Blessed Virgin Mary,
whom he had chosen as his Mother,
should be our Mother also,
graciously grant, we pray,
that we, who fly to her protection,
may find comfort by invoking our Mother's name.
Through our Lord Jesus Christ, your Son,
who lives and reigns with you in the unity of the Holy Spirit,
God, for ever and ever.

PRAYER OVER THE OFFERINGS

Lord,
look with favor on the gifts we offer
and grant that our hearts may be enlightened
by the Holy Spirit,
so that in imitation of Blessed Mary ever-Virgin,
we may seek to be faithful to Christ, your Son,
to please him in all that we do,
and to live only for him.
Who lives and reigns for ever and ever.

Preface P 21, page 105.

Communion Antiphon Cf. Luke 1:48

All generations will call me blessed,
for God has looked on his lowly handmaid.

PRAYER AFTER COMMUNION

Grant us we pray, O Lord,
whom you have strengthened at the table of word and Sacrament,
that, with Blessed Mary as our patron and guide,
we may reject whatever is contrary to the name of Christian
and follow whatever accords with it.
Through Christ our Lord.

22. HOLY MARY, HANDMAID OF THE LORD

In the Gospel according to Luke the Blessed Virgin twice describes herself as "the handmaid of the Lord": when she gives her consent to the message of the Angel (cf. Luke 1:38), and when she proclaims the greatness of the Lord because of "the great things" he has worked in her (cf. Luke 1:49). To understand fully the meaning and force of her title of "handmaid of the Lord" we must read it in the light of the songs of the "Servant of the Lord" (cf. Isaiah 42:1-7; 49:1-9; 50:1-11; 52:1—53:12), and above all in the light of Jesus Christ as the one who fulfills the figure of the "Servant of the Lord": he "did not come to be served, but to serve, and to give his life as a ransom for many" (Mark 10:45).

The Blessed Virgin is honored liturgically under the title of "handmaid of the Lord" in certain religious institutes, especially in the Congregation of the Passion of Jesus Christ (Passionists). Most of the texts of this Mass are taken from its *Proprium missarum*, General Curia CP, Rome, 1974, pp. 30-31.

This Mass celebrates the merciful plan of salvation by which God chooses the Blessed Virgin, his lowly handmaid, to be Mother and partner of Christ (cf. Col). As the Second Vatican Council teaches, Mary, "the daughter of Adam, in giving her consent to the word of God, became the Mother of Jesus. Embracing wholeheartedly the saving will of God and being unhindered by any sin, she devoted herself completely as the handmaid of the Lord to the person and work of her Son. In subordination to him and with him, by the grace of almighty God she served the mystery of redemption" (LG, no. 56).

The Blessed Virgin, the lowly handmaid of the Lord, is therefore addressed as the "servant of your love" (Pref), giving herself completely to God's service (cf. PO) and to the work of the Son for the salvation of all (cf. Pref).

The Mass closely follows the teaching of the Gospel in celebrating Mary, the lowly handmaid, as also raised to royal dignity: she who "gave great service to Christ" was given great honor by the Father (cf. Pref, John 12:26); "she who saw herself as [God's] lowly handmaid was raised up" by God to "reign as queen in glory in the presence" of his Son (Pref). This is well expressed in the *Alleluia* verse: "Blessed are you, O Virgin Mary, you declared yourself the handmaid of the Lord, and now, exalted above the choirs of Angels, you are acclaimed by the Church as Queen of heaven."

Entrance Antiphon Luke 1:47-48

My spirit rejoices in God my Savior,
because the Lord has looked on his lowly handmaid.

COLLECT

Lord our God,
in your loving plan of redemption
you chose the Blessed Virgin,
your lowly handmaid,
to be the Mother and companion of Christ your Son;
grant that by constantly looking up to her
we may give you wholehearted service
in untiring care for the salvation of the world.
Through our Lord Jesus Christ, your Son,
who lives and reigns with you in the unity of the Holy Spirit,
God, for ever and ever.

PRAYER OVER THE OFFERINGS

All-holy Father,
on this memorial of the Blessed Virgin Mary,
your obedient and devoted handmaid,
receive our offerings and gifts
and grant that we may present to you ourselves
as a sacrifice pleasing in your sight.
Through Christ our Lord.

Preface P 22, page 106.

Communion Antiphon Psalm 86:15-16

Lord God, look upon me and have pity on me;
save the child of your handmaid.

PRAYER AFTER COMMUNION

Having been made partakers of this spiritual food,
we pray, O Lord our God,
that, steadily imitating the Blessed Virgin Mary,
we may always be found intent on service of the Church
and may know the joys of doing your will.
Through Christ our Lord.

23. THE BLESSED VIRGIN MARY, TEMPLE OF THE LORD

The "mystery of the temple" was fulfilled in Christ Jesus (cf. John 2:19-22), in whom "dwells the whole fullness of the deity bodily" (Colossians 2:9). In Scripture the Church too is called a "holy temple"; "you are fellow citizens with the holy ones and members of the household of God, built upon the foundation of the apostles and prophets, with Christ Jesus himself as the captstone. Through him the whole structure is held together and grows into *temple sacred* in the Lord" (Ephesians 2:19-21). Individual Christians are also "a temple of God" because God dwells in their hearts: "Do you not know that you are the *temple of God*, and that the Spirit of God dwells in you? . . . for the temple of God, which you are, is holy" (1 Corinthians 3:16-17).

In a unique way the Blessed Virgin is herself "a holy temple":

—when she conceived the very Son of God in her immaculate womb, she became a true temple of the true God;

—when she cherished the word of God in her heart (cf. Luke 2:19, 51), loved Christ so ardently, and faithfully kept his word, the Son and the Father came to her and made their home with her, in accordance with the promise of the Lord (cf. John 14:23).

This Mass therefore celebrates the divine motherhood of our Lady and her holiness of life under this image of "the temple."

Our Lady is called "a holy temple" built "with artistry beyond all telling" by God for the Son (Col); a "temple" of God's glory "without compare," because of her "obedience of faith and the mystery of the Incarnation" (Pref); a "temple of holiness and temple of love for us sinners . . . temple filled with the Holy Spirit" (*All*).

Other images are also used to draw out the significance of the Blessed Virgin Mary, all more or less equivalent to the idea of the "temple": *a tabernacle* within which God dwells, a dwelling that will always stand firm (Com Ant, Psalm 46:5-6; Ent Ant, Revelation 21:3); *a house of the Lord*, which God has filled with his presence (cf. 1 Read, 1 Kings 8:11; Resp, Psalm 84:11); *a house of gold*, "adorned by the Spirit with every kind of virtue" (Pref); *a royal palace*, "resplendent with the presence of the One who is the Truth" (Pref), dwelt in by the King of kings; *the holy city*, "rejoicing in its streams of grace" (Pref, cf. Psalm 46:5); *the ark of the covenant*, "enshrining the author of the New Law" (Pref).

Entrance Antiphon Revelation 21:3

I heard a great voice from the throne:
"Here God lives among the human race!
He will dwell with them, and they will be his people,
and God will be with them as their God."

COLLECT

Lord God,
with artistry beyond all telling
you fashioned a holy temple for your Son
in the virginal womb of Blessed Mary;
grant that, in faithfully safeguarding the grace of our Baptism,
we may worship you in spirit and in truth
and become like Mary a temple of your glory.
Through our Lord Jesus Christ, your Son,
who lives and reigns with you in the unity of the Holy Spirit,
God, for ever and ever.

PRAYER OVER THE OFFERINGS

Lord, receive these gifts from our grateful hearts
as we celebrate this memorial of the Blessed Virgin Mary,
from whose life we learn the secret of prayer and praise.
In your goodness grant that like her
we may offer you a sacrifice of holiness
by doing always what is pleasing in your sight.
Through Christ our Lord.

Preface P 23, page 107.

Communion Antiphon Cf. Psalm 46:5-6

Blessed are you, Virgin Mary, holy tabernacle of the ways stand firm.

PRAYER AFTER COMMUNION

**Lord our God,
you have nourished us with food and drink from heaven;
grant that, like the Blessed Virgin Mary,
we may serve you in holiness of life,
revere your presence in our neighbor,
and with Mary proclaim your greatness
with sincerity of heart.
Through Christ our Lord.**

24. THE BLESSED VIRGIN MARY, SEAT OF WISDOM

Beginning with the tenth century we find in Masses of our Lady, Mother of the Incarnate Wisdom of God, that readings are often from the Wisdom literature (or "sapiential epistles"), especially Sirach and Proverbs (cf. OLM 707:5, 6). In these texts the Church, though listening primarily to the voice of eternal Wisdom, hears also the voice of the Blessed Virgin Mary, for in them, according to the common understanding of the medieval writers, the Wisdom of God speaks in a certain sense "in the person of the Virgin."

From the twelfth century, at Morning Prayer (Lauds) and in litanies in honor of our Lady, a number of titles are given her in praise of her close relationship with eternal Wisdom: *"mother of Wisdom," "fountain of Wisdom," "house of Wisdom," "seat of Wisdom,"* of which the last became the most common.

Under this title the Blessed Virgin is honored, even in liturgical celebrations, in particular Churches, in universities, and in religious institutes, especially the Missionaries of the Company of Mary, founded by St. Louis Grignion de Montfort (d. 1716). The Mass formulary given here, except for the Preface, is taken from the *Proprium missarum* of the Missionaries of the Company of Mary.

The title "seat of Wisdom" celebrates the maternal role of our Lady, her royal dignity, and her incomparable wisdom and prudence in the things of God:

—*her maternal role*, because through the mystery of the Incarnation the Wisdom of the Father is cradled in the arms of his Virgin Mother;

—*her royal dignity*, because the child sitting on Mary's lap is the messianic King, who will be called "Son of the Most High," to whom "the Lord God will give the throne of David his father, and he will rule over the house of Jacob for ever, and of his kingdom there will be no end" (Luke 1:32-33; cf. Isaiah 9:6-7); he is the King visited by the wise men coming from afar, who find him with his Mother and adore him, offering him royal gifts (cf. Matthew 2:1-12).

—*her wisdom and prudence*, because our Lady is seen in the Gospel as a "wise Virgin," who has chosen the better part, like Mary of Bethany (cf. Luke 10:42), a "teacher of truth," who hands on to the Church the saving deeds and words of her Son, which she has treasured in her heart (cf. Luke 2:19, 51); St. Bruno of Asti (d. 1123) writes: "Mother most wise, alone most worthy of such a Son! She kept all these words in her heart, preserving them for us and commending them to our remembrance, so that afterwards, through her teaching them, recounting them, proclaiming them, they might be recorded, preached throughout the world, and announced to all nations" (*Commentaria in Lucam*, pars I, cap. II: PL 165:355).

Entrance Antiphon

Blessed are you, holy Mary, wisest of virgins:
the Word of truth was cradled in your arms;
blessed are you, most prudent of virgins:
you have chosen the better part.

COLLECT

A All-holy Father, eternal God,
in your goodness
you prepared a royal throne for your Wisdom
in the womb of the Blessed Virgin Mary;
bathe your Church
in the radiance of your life-giving Word,
that, pressing forward on its pilgrim way
in the light of your truth,
it may come to the joy
of a perfect knowledge of your love.
Through our Lord Jesus Christ, your Son,
who lives and reigns with you in the unity of the Holy Spirit,
God, for ever and ever.

B God of wisdom,
in your desire to restore us to your friendship
after we had lost it by sin,
you chose the Blessed Virgin Mary
as the seat of your Wisdom.
Grant through her intercession
that we may not seek the wisdom of the proud
but with humility treasure your revealed wisdom.
Through our Lord Jesus Christ, your Son,
who lives and reigns with you in the unity of the Holy Spirit,
God, for ever and ever.

PRAYER OVER THE OFFERINGS

**Lord, sanctify these gifts that we offer you,
and through the intercession
of the Virgin Mary in her glory
prepare in our hearts
a worthy dwelling for your Wisdom.
Through Christ our Lord.**

Preface P 24, page 108.

Communion Antiphon — Proverbs 9:5, 6b

**Come, eat my bread,
drink the wine I have prepared for you;
walk in the way of wisdom.**

PRAYER AFTER COMMUNION

**Lord our God,
through this holy sacrifice
pour into our hearts
the light of wisdom
which so wonderfully filled
the heart of the Virgin Mother,
so that we may know you in truth
and love you with fidelity.
Through Christ our Lord.**

25. THE BLESSED VIRGIN MARY, IMAGE AND MOTHER OF THE CHURCH

I

On 21 November 1964, at the end of the third session of the Second Vatican Council, Paul VI, during the celebration of Mass, declared our Lady "Mother of the Church, that is, of the entire Christian people, both the faithful and their pastors, who call her their most loving Mother," and decreed that "from now onward the whole Christian people should give even greater honor to the Mother of God under this most loving title" (AAS 56 [1965], p. 1015).

Accordingly, many particular Churches and religious families began to venerate the Blessed Virgin under the title of "Mother of the Church." In 1974, to encourage Marian celebrations during the Holy Year of Reconciliation (1975), this Mass was composed; it was shortly afterwards inserted in the second *editio typica* of *The Roman Missal* among the Votive Masses in honor of the Blessed Virgin Mary.

The formulary looks at the many links between the Church and the Blessed Virgin but celebrates in particular the maternal role which God has been pleased to assign to our Lady in the Church and for the sake of the Church.

The euchological texts are especially concerned with four key events in the history of salvation:

—*the Incarnation of the Word*, when Mary received the Son of God "in her Immaculate Heart, she was found worthy to conceive him in her virgin's womb and, giving birth to the Creator, she nurtured the beginnings of the Church" (Pref);

—*the Passion of Christ*, when, "as he hung upon the Cross, chose the Blessed Virgin Mary, his Mother, to be our Mother also" (Col, cf. Pref, Com Ant, A);

—*the outpouring of the Holy Spirit at Pentecost*, when the Mother of the Lord "joined her supplication to the prayers of the disciples and so became the pattern of the Church at prayer" (Pref);

—*the Assumption of our Lady:* in the "glory of heaven, she accompanies your pilgrim Church with a mother's love and watches in kindness over the Church's homeward steps, until the Lord's Day shall come in glorious splendor" (Pref).

Entrance Antiphon Cf. Acts 1:14

The disciples devoted themselves with one accord to prayer
with Mary, the Mother of Jesus.

COLLECT

O God, Father of mercies,
whose Only Begotten Son, as he hung upon the Cross,
chose the Blessed Virgin Mary, his Mother,
to be our Mother also,
grant, we pray, that with her loving help
your Church may be more fruitful day by day
and, exulting in the holiness of her children,
may draw to her embrace all the families of the peoples.
Through our Lord Jesus Christ, your Son,
who lives and reigns with you in the unity of the Holy Spirit,
God, for ever and ever.

PRAYER OVER THE OFFERINGS

Receive our offerings, O Lord,
and transform them into the mystery of salvation,
so that by its power we may be set aflame
with the charity of the Virgin Mary, Mother of the Church,
and with her may be united more closely
to the work of redemption.
Through Christ our Lord.

Preface P 25, page 109.

Communion Antiphon

A As he hung upon the Cross, Cf. John 19:26-27
Jesus said to the disciple whom he loved:
Behold your mother.

B Blessed are you, Mary, full of grace,
mother and virgin;
you are a shining example of faith, hope, and love to the Church.

PRAYER AFTER COMMUNION

Having received the pledge of redemption and of life,
we humbly pray, O Lord,
that, with the Blessed Virgin's motherly help,
your Church may teach all nations
by proclaiming the Gospel
and, through the grace of the outpouring of the Spirit,
fill the whole earth.
Through Christ our Lord.

26. THE BLESSED VIRGIN MARY, IMAGE AND MOTHER OF THE CHURCH

II

This Mass is in celebration of God the Father, who in his "infinite goodness" (Pref) has given the Church the Blessed Virgin Mary, the Mother of Christ, as a "model of every virtue" (Ent Ant, Com Ant, cf. LG, no. 65). "Although in the Blessed Virgin the Church already attains that perfection by which she exists without spot or wrinkle (cf. Ephesians 5:27), the faithful are still striving to conquer sin and grow in holiness. They therefore raise their eyes to Mary, who shines brightly as the exemplar of virtues for the whole company of the elect" (LG, no. 65):

—*the model of sublime love,* so that the faithful pray: that the Church "may stand before all peoples as the Sacrament of [God's] love" (Col);

—*the model of faith and hope,* so that the faithful ask that the Church "may look always to the Blessed Virgin and so grow in fervor of faith," and be "strengthened by the hope of future glory" (PC);

—*the model of profound humility:* ". . . [God has] shown us in the Blessed Virgin Mary the model of . . . profound humility" (Col);

—*the model of persevering prayer in oneness of mind and heart,* for the Apostles and the first disciples "devoted themselves with one accord to prayer, together with . . . Mary, the Mother of Jesus" (1 Read, Acts 1:12-14); Mary "prays with the Apostles in oneness of mind and heart" (Pref);

—*the model of worship in spirit:* Mary is "the shining model of true worship for [God's] Church and of our duty to offer ourselves as a holy victim, pleasing in [God's] eyes" (PO, cf. Romans 12:1);

—*the model of liturgical worship:* the Mother of Jesus, as Pope Paul VI reminds us, is the "exemplar of that sense of reverent devotion with which the Church celebrates the divine mysteries and expresses them in its life" (MC, no. 16); for Mary is "the Virgin who listens, . . . the Virgin of prayer, . . . the Virgin Mother, . . . the Virgin who offers" (Pref; cf. MC, nos. 16–21); she is the Virgin who keeps vigil, awaiting the Resurrection of her Son (cf. Pref). In brief, Mary is "the model of the Church as a whole in its worship of God" (MC, no. 21).

Entrance Antiphon

**You are truly worthy of all praise, holy Virgin Mary;
you are the Mother of Christ, our God;
you set before the Church a shining model of every virtue!**

COLLECT

**Lord God,
you have shown us in the Blessed Virgin Mary
the model of sublime love and profound humility;
grant that your Church may be like her,
obedient to your commandment of love,
so that by giving itself wholeheartedly
to seeking your glory and to serving others
it may stand before all peoples
as the Sacrament of your love.
Through our Lord Jesus Christ, your Son,
who lives and reigns with you in the unity of the Holy Spirit,
God, for ever and ever.**

PRAYER OVER THE OFFERINGS

**Lord, transform these gifts,
which we bring to you with joyful hearts,
into the Sacrament of our salvation
on this memorial of the Virgin Mary in glory;
for she is the shining model
of true worship for your Church
and of our duty to offer ourselves
as a holy victim, pleasing in your eyes.
Through Christ our Lord.**

Preface P 26, page 110.

Communion Antiphon

Blessed are you, Mary, full of grace:
we lift up our eyes to you as a shining model of every virtue
to the whole company of those whom God has chosen!

PRAYER AFTER COMMUNION

Lord God, we have offered to you in sacrifice
the holy mysteries of your table
and have received with loving hearts
the Body and Blood of your Son;
grant that your Church
may look always to the Blessed Virgin
and so grow in fervor of faith,
be confirmed in love,
and be strengthened by the hope of future glory.
Through Christ our Lord.

27. THE BLESSED VIRGIN MARY, IMAGE AND MOTHER OF THE CHURCH

III

This Mass celebrates God's goodness in loving the Church so much that the Blessed Virgin is set before its eyes as the prophetic image of its pilgrimage on earth and of its future glory in heaven. In the words of the Second Vatican Council, "in her the Church holds up and admires the most excellent effect of the redemption and joyfully contemplates, as in a flawless image, that which the Church itself desires and hopes wholly to be" (SC, art. 103).

The Blessed Virgin, as "the spotless mirror of God's glory" (Com Ant, A, cf. Wisdom 7:26; cf. Ent Ant), provides the Church with a most faithful image of the perfect disciple, the pure virgin, the faithful bride, the loving mother, the queen crowned with glory. The liturgy therefore celebrates the Blessed Virgin as:

—*the disciple* who is perfect in the following of Christ. We pray then that the Church, "with eyes fixed on Mary, . . . may follow closely in the footsteps of her Son" (Col), and be fashioned more and more "in that image of Christ, which it admires and praises in his glorious Mother" (PO);

—"*a virgin* unsurpassed in purity of faith" (Pref), whom the Church always strives to imitate: for "she is herself a virgin who keeps whole and unsullied the faith she has given to her Bridegroom" (LG, no. 64);

—"*a bride* joined to Christ in an unbreakable bond of love and united with him in his suffering" (Pref); as the Church "contemplates her in the light of the Word truly made flesh" it reverently enters more deeply into the surpassing mystery of the Incarnation and takes on more and more the image of its Bridegroom" (LG, no. 65);

—"*a mother* by the overshadowing of the Holy Spirit, filled with loving concern for all her children" (Pref); the Church, by "imitating her love and faithfully carrying out the will of the Father and through the word of God it has faithfully received, itself becomes a mother. For by preaching and Baptism it brings forth to new and immortal life children conceived by the Holy Spirit and born of God" (LG, no. 64);

—"*a queen* adorned with the jewels of grace, . . . sharing eternally in the glory of her Lord" (Pref); "as the Church looks on [Mary] it sees the perfect image of its future glory" (Ent Ant, cf. SC, art. 103; cf. PO, Pref).

Entrance Antiphon

Hail, holy Mary, mirror without stain!
As the Church looks on you it sees
the perfect image of its future glory.

COLLECT

Lord our God, through your power and goodness
the Blessed Virgin,
the fairest fruit of your redeeming love,
shines forth as the perfect image of the Church;
grant to your people on their pilgrim way on earth
that, with eyes fixed on Mary,
they may follow closely in the footsteps of her Son
until they come to that fullness of glory,
which now they contemplate in his Mother
with hearts filled with joy.
Through our Lord Jesus Christ, your Son,
who lives and reigns with you in the unity of the Holy Spirit,
God, for ever and ever.

PRAYER OVER THE OFFERINGS

May this oblation dedicated to your name
purify us, O Lord,
and fashion your Church more and more
in that image of Christ,
which it admires and praises in his glorious Mother.
Through Christ our Lord.

Preface P 27, page 112.

Communion Antiphon

A **Virgin Mary, you are the brightness of eternal light,** Cf. Wisdom 7:26
the spotless mirror of God's glory, the image of his goodness.

B **Behold, you will conceive in your womb and bear a son,** Luke 1:31
and you shall name him Jesus.

PRAYER AFTER COMMUNION

**Grant to your Church, O Lord,
that, strengthened by the power of this Sacrament,
she may eagerly walk in the pathways of the Gospel,
until she reaches the blessed vision of peace,
which the Virgin Mary, your lowly handmaid,
already enjoys eternally in glory.
Through Christ our Lord.**

28. THE IMMACULATE HEART OF THE BLESSED VIRGIN MARY

The Roman Liturgy celebrates the Memorial of the Immaculate Heart of the Blessed Virgin Mary with a special formulary on the Saturday after the second Sunday after Pentecost. Several Masses, however, are to be found in honor of the Immaculate Heart of Mary in the propers of Masses of particular Churches and religious institutes, celebrating different aspects of this devotion. The formulary set out here is largely drawn from the *Proprium Congregationis Missionariorum Filiorum Immaculati Cordis beatae Virginis* (cf. *Annales Congregationis* 52, 1976, pp. 363–365).

The meaning of "the heart of the Virgin" is to be understood in a biblical sense: it denotes the person of the Blessed Virgin herself; her intimate and unique being; the center and source of her interior life, of her mind and memory, of her will and love; the single-mindedness with which she loved God and the disciples and devoted herself wholeheartedly to the saving work of her Son.

The formulary celebrates the loving kindness of God, who, after giving to the Church the heart of our Lord Jesus Christ as a proof of his love, gave it also the heart of the Blessed Virgin Mary to be contemplated as the model of the "new heart" of one who lives by the "new Covenant."

The heart of the Blessed Virgin, who, filled with faith and love, received the Word of God, is called in the first place the "home of [God's] eternal Word" (Col), and the "sanctuary of the Holy Spirit" (Col, cf. LG, no. 53), because of the divine Spirit dwelling always within her. It is described as *"Immaculate"* (Col), that is, free from the stain of sin; as *"wise"* (Pref), because the Blessed Virgin, linking prophecy to fact, treasured in her heart the memory of the words and deeds belonging to the mystery of salvation (cf. Luke 2:19, 51); as *"obedient"* (Pref, cf. 1 Kings 3:9), because her heart willingly united itself to the will of God (cf. Luke 1:48); as *"new"* (Pref), in accordance with the prophecy of Ezekiel (cf. Ezekiel 18:31; 36:26), clothed in the newness of grace through the anticipated merits of Christ (cf. Ephesians 4:23-24); as *"gentle"* (Pref), like the heart of Christ as he invites us: "Learn from me, for I am gentle and humble of heart" (Matthew 11:29); as *"undivided"* (Pref), that is, free from all duplicity and imbued with the Spirit of truth; as *"pure"* (Pref) or, as in the Beatitudes (cf. Matthew 5:8), capable of seeing God; as *"steadfast"* (Pref) in embracing the will of God, when, as Simeon prophesied (cf. Luke 2:35), persecution threatened her Son (cf. Matthew 2:13) or his Death was imminent (cf. John 19:25); as *"watchful"* (Pref), for, like the heart of the beloved in the Song of Songs (cf. 5:2), when Christ lay asleep in the sepulcher, her heart kept vigil, waiting for his Resurrection.

Entrance Antiphon Sirach 24:25

In me is all the grace of the way and the truth,
in me is all hope of life and of strength.

COLLECT

Lord our God,
you made the Immaculate Heart of the Blessed Virgin Mary
the home of your eternal Word
and the sanctuary of the Holy Spirit.
Give us a heart that is free from sin
and attentive to your will,
that, faithful to your commandments,
we may love you above all things
and seek to help others in their need.
Through our Lord Jesus Christ, your Son,
who lives and reigns with you in the unity of the Holy Spirit,
God, for ever and ever.

PRAYER OVER THE OFFERINGS

Lord, look with favor on the gifts we bring
as we celebrate this memorial
of the Blessed Virgin Mary;
grant that, as we follow her example,
we may faithfully cherish and continually ponder
the riches of grace that we owe to your Son.
Who lives and reigns for ever and ever.

Preface P 28, page 113.

Communion Antiphon Luke 2:19

Mary treasured all these words,
reflecting on them in her heart.

PRAYER AFTER COMMUNION

Having been made partakers of eternal redemption,
we pray, O Lord,
that we, who commemorate the Mother of your Son,
may glory in the fullness of your grace
and experience its continued increase for our salvation.
Through Christ our Lord.

29. THE BLESSED VIRGIN MARY, QUEEN OF ALL CREATION

In 1954 the Feast of the Queenship of Mary was instituted by Pius XII, to be celebrated on 31 May. In 1969 Paul VI, promulgating the new General Roman Calendar, appropriately transferred the feast to 22 August, the octave of the Assumption. The royal dignity of our Lady is part of the mystery of her full glorification and perfect conformity with her Son, the King of all the ages. In the words of the Second Vatican Council, "the Immaculate Virgin, . . . when she had completed her earthly life, was taken up body and soul into the glory of heaven and exalted as the *queen of all creation*, so that she might be more fully conformed to her Son, the Lord of lords (cf. Revelation 19:16) and victor over sin and death" (LG, no. 59).

As the kingdom of Christ "does not belong to this world" (John 18:36), so too the royal dignity of our Lady does not belong to the order of nature, but to that of grace. Among the qualities that make up her royal dignity in the order of grace the texts of the Mass celebrate four in particular: her humility, her role as mother, her earnest intercession, her function as a sign of the future glory of the Church.

Our Lady is *the queen gloriously reigning* in heaven, because she was on earth the lowly handmaid (cf. Luke 1:38, 48): in the words of our Lord, "the one who humbles himself will be exalted" (Luke 14:11). As God the Father has crowned Christ with glory and honor (cf. Pref; Psalm 8:6), after he humbled himself even to accepting death (cf. Pref; Philippians 2:8), and as he has seated him at his right hand (cf. Pref; Psalm 8:6), so he has exalted his lowly handmaid above all the choirs of Angels (cf. Pref).

She is *queen and Mother*, because she became the Mother of the messianic King, who sits on "David's throne and over his kingdom" (Isaiah 9:6; cf. 1 Read, Isaiah 9:1-3, 5-6; Gos, Luke 1:26-38); and, by the will of God, she is our Mother also, as the Church testifies: "O God, [you] made the Mother of your Son to be our Mother and Queen" (Col).

She is *the queen who intercedes*, exalted "above all the choirs of Angels," reigning in glory with her Son, interceding for all God's children, our advocate of grace, and the queen of all creation (Pref; cf. LG, no. 62).

She is *the queen who is the sign of the Church in its future glory*, because what has been accomplished in her as a member surpassing all others will be accomplished in all the members of Christ's Mystical Body. It is right, therefore, for the Church to ask the intercession of our Lady that its members may share "in the heavenly Kingdom the glory promised to [God's] children" (Col).

The formulary of this Mass is taken from *The Roman Missal*, 22 August; the Preface echoes the prayer for the crowning of an image of our Lady (cf. *Order of Crowning an Image of the Blessed Virgin Mary*, English ed., pp. 15–16).

Entrance Antiphon Psalm 45:10

At your right stands the queen in robes of gold,
finely arrayed.

COLLECT

O God, who made the Mother of your Son
to be our Mother and our Queen,
graciously grant that,
sustained by her intercession,
we may attain in the heavenly Kingdom
the glory promised to your children.
Through our Lord Jesus Christ, your Son,
who lives and reigns with you in the unity of the Holy Spirit,
God, for ever and ever.

PRAYER OVER THE OFFERINGS

As we observe this memorial of the Blessed Virgin Mary,
we bring you our offerings, O Lord,
praying to be given strength by the humanity of Christ,
who offered himself to you on the Cross
as the unblemished oblation.
Who lives and reigns for ever and ever.

Preface P 29, page 114.

Communion Antiphon Cf. Luke 1:45

Blessed are you who have believed
that what was spoken to you by the Lord would be fulfilled.

PRAYER AFTER COMMUNION

Having received this heavenly Sacrament,
we humbly pray, O Lord,
that we, who reverently celebrate the Memorial of the Blessed Virgin Mary,
may merit to be partakers at your eternal banquet.
Through Christ our Lord.

SECTION 2

This section contains nine Mass formularies for the celebration of a memorial of the Mother of the Lord under titles that refer to her cooperation in fostering the spiritual life of the faithful.

MASS FORMULARIES

30. The Blessed Virgin Mary, Mother and Mediatrix of Grace
31. The Blessed Virgin Mary, Fountain of Salvation
32. The Blessed Virgin Mary, Mother and Teacher in the Spirit
33. The Blessed Virgin Mary, Mother of Good Counsel
34. The Blessed Virgin Mary, Cause of Our Joy
35. The Blessed Virgin Mary, Pillar of Faith
36. The Blessed Virgin Mary, Mother of Fairest Love
37. The Blessed Virgin Mary, Mother of Divine Hope
38. Holy Mary, Mother of Unity

30. THE BLESSED VIRGIN MARY, MOTHER AND MEDIATRIX OF GRACE

In 1921 Pope Benedict XV (d. 1922), at the request of Cardinal Désiré Joseph Mercier (d. 1926), granted the whole of Belgium an Office and Mass of the Blessed Virgin Mary, Mediatrix of All Graces, to be celebrated on 31 May. This Office and Mass were extended by the Holy See to many other dioceses and religious institutes at their own request, so that the commemoration of our Lady as mediatrix became almost universal.

The Second Vatican Council in 1964 treated at some length the role of our Lady in the mystery of Christ and of the Church and gave a careful explanation of the meaning and force of her "mediation": "The maternal role of Mary in relation to the human family in no way obscures or lessens the unique mediation of Christ but rather demonstrates its power. Any saving influence of the Blessed Virgin on men and women is due not to any intrinsic necessity but to God's good pleasure. It flows from the superabundance of Christ's merits, is founded on his mediation, is entirely dependent on it, and from it derives its whole efficacy. It does not in any way impede but rather fosters the immediate union of the faithful with Christ" (LG, no. 60).

In 1971 the Congregation for Divine Worship approved a Mass of the Blessed Virgin Mary, Mother and Mediatrix of Grace. This Mass, faithfully following the teaching of the Second Vatican Council, commemorates both the maternal role of our Lady and her function of mediation (cf. *Proprium missarum Ordinis Fratrum Servorum beatae Mariae Virginis*, Curia Generalis OSM, Rome, 1972, pp. 36–37). Currently this Mass is celebrated in many places on 8 May, and, with some changes and the addition of a Preface, is set out here.

The formulary rightly gives pride of place to Christ, "truly God and truly human . . . the one Mediator . . . always living to make intercession for us" (Pref; cf. 1 Timothy 2:5; Hebrews 7:25; PO, PC). It also commemorates our Lady as "Mother of the author of all grace," for God the Father, in his "eternal wisdom and love" (Col; cf. Pref), chose her as "the Mother and companion of the Redeemer" (Col, Pref).

—The Virgin Mary is *Mother of grace*, for in her "chaste womb" she carried him who is "truly God and truly human" (Ent Ant, A), and brought forth for us "the author of all grace" (Col; cf. *All*).

—The Virgin Mary is *mediatrix of grace*, for she was the handmaid of Christ in gaining for us the greatest of all graces: redemption and salvation, the divine life and unending glory (cf. LG, no. 61).

In the formulary the "mediation" of our Lady is correctly interpreted as "the love that she bestows as a mother" (Pref): "of intercession and pardon, of prayer and grace, of reconciliation and peace" (Pref).

Entrance Antiphon

A Hail, holy Mary, rich fountain of love, treasure-house of all graces,
in your chaste womb you bore him who is truly God and truly human.

B Hail, holy Mother of God, our life was lost
but now through you it is restored,
for you received a child from heaven
and brought to birth the Savior of the world.

COLLECT

Lord our God,
in your eternal wisdom and love
you chose the Blessed Virgin Mary
to be the Mother of the author of all grace
and as his companion in bringing about
the mystery of our redemption.
Grant that she may obtain for us
graces in abundance
and lead us at last
to the harbor of eternal salvation.
Through our Lord Jesus Christ, your Son,
who lives and reigns with you in the unity of the Holy Spirit,
God, for ever and ever.

PRAYER OVER THE OFFERINGS

Lord,
receive our offering of peace and praise
on this memorial of the Virgin Mary in glory;
by the power of the Holy Spirit
make what we present the Sacrament of our redemption,
so that what Christ our Mediator has established
as the means of our reconciliation with you
may become for us the source of grace
and the enduring fountain of eternal salvation.
Through Christ our Lord.

Preface P 30, page 115.

Communion Antiphon Revelation 22:17

The Spirit and the Bride say: Come.
Let all who hear say: Come. Let all who thirst, come;
let all who will, take the free gift of the water of life.

PRAYER AFTER COMMUNION

Refreshed, Lord God,
at the fountain of salvation,
we pray that by the power of this Sacrament
and through the prayers of the Blessed Virgin
we may be more closely united
to Christ, the Mediator,
and ever more faithfully enter into
the mystery of redemption.
Through Christ our Lord.

31. THE BLESSED VIRGIN MARY, FOUNTAIN OF SALVATION

The Mother of the Lord is frequently honored under the title of "fountain" in the liturgies of East and West. She is called "fountain of living water," "fountain of charity," "fountain of clemency," "fountain of grace," "fountain of mercy," "fountain sealed" (cf. 1 Read, Song of Songs 4:12), "fountain of salvation" (cf. G. G. Meersseman, *Der Hymnos Akathistos im Abendland*, vol. 2, Universitätsverlag, Freiburg, Switzerland, 1960, pp. 309–310).

There are a number of sanctuaries dedicated to our Lady under the title of "fountain," often with a spring of water used by the faithful on pilgrimage. The most celebrated of these in the East is the sanctuary of the Mother of God of the Living Fountain in Constantinople, erected in the sixth century. In the West there is the sanctuary at Lourdes, beside the cave where our Lady appeared to St. Bernadette Soubirous and caused a spring of water to gush forth.

This formulary celebrates:

—*the divine motherhood of our Lady*, for it was through her that God opened for us "the fountain of salvation" (Col): "in the great mystery of the Incarnation . . . she brought forth [God's] eternal Word, Jesus Christ, the fountain of living water" (Pref). He is the true temple of God (cf. John 2:21), from which the saving waters come forth, healing all whom they touch (cf. 1 Read, Ezekiel 47:1-2, 8-9, 12); he invites the thirsty to come to him and drink (cf. Com Ant, A, John 7:37), that is, those who believe in him are to receive the gift of the Holy Spirit (cf. John 7:39); he is the rock (cf. 1 Corinthians 10:4), struck by the lance, from which "immediately blood and water flowed out" (Gos, John 19:25-37).

—*the spiritual maternity of the Church:* for the Church, as a wise mother, satisfies the thirst of the faithful by giving them "the waters flowing from Christ's side. These are the rich, life-giving waters served in the Sacraments" (Pref), especially in the Eucharistic banquet, at which the faithful draw "water in joy from the fountain of the Savior" (PC, cf. Resp, Isaiah 12:3), and "the Sacrament we [they] have received" becomes "a spring of water welling up to eternal life" (PC);

—the outpouring of the Holy Spirit, which is frequently symbolized in Scripture as the outpouring of water. The Entrance Antiphon (A) recalls the words of Isaiah: "I will pour out water upon the thirsty ground . . . I will pour out my spirit upon your offspring, my blessing upon your descendants" (cf. Isaiah 44:3). The fountain from which the water flows is Christ himself (as in the Collect, "grant that we who celebrate the memory of our Lady may always draw from this wellspring of life and bring forth a rich harvest of the fruits of the Holy Spirit") and the Sacraments instituted by [Christ], by which the faithful as they receive them are "filled with the Holy Spirit" (Pref).

Several texts of this formulary, and the alternative readings for the liturgy of the word, are taken from the *Proprio de la misa y de la liturgia de las horas de la diócesis de Cartagena*, Cartagena, 1985, pp. 32–34.

Entrance Antiphon

A I will pour water over the thirsty land, Cf. Isaiah 44:3-4
I will pour my Spirit on your descendants, my blessing on your children, and they will grow like poplars beside flowing streams.

B The streams of a river make glad the city of God, Psalm 46:5-6a
the holy dwelling-place of the Most High. God is within the city;
it will remain unshaken for ever.

COLLECT

All-holy Lord and Father,
through the Blessed Virgin Mary
you have unsealed for us the fountain of salvation,
Jesus Christ, your Son;
grant that we who celebrate the memory of our Lady
may always draw from this wellspring of life
and bring forth a rich harvest
of the fruits of the Holy Spirit.
Through our Lord Jesus Christ, your Son,
who lives and reigns with you in the unity of the Holy Spirit,
God, for ever and ever.

PRAYER OVER THE OFFERINGS

Lord, change into the Sacrament of salvation
the gifts we joyously present
on this memorial of the most holy Virgin Mary,
for it was through her intercession
that your Son worked the first of his great signs,
changing an abundance of water into wine.
Through Christ our Lord.

Preface P 31, page 116.

Communion Antiphon

A Let anyone who thirsts and believes in me, says the Lord, John 7:37
come to me and drink.

B All you that thirst, come to the waters; Isaiah 55:1
buy and eat, come, buy wine and milk,
without payment, without cost.

PRAYER AFTER COMMUNION

Lord God, you have refreshed us
at your banquet of salvation
where we have drawn water in joy
from the fountain of the Savior;
grant that as we celebrate the memory of Blessed Mary
the Sacrament we have received
may be a spring of water welling up to eternal life.
Through Christ our Lord.

32. THE BLESSED VIRGIN MARY, MOTHER AND TEACHER IN THE SPIRIT

The Carmelite brothers and sisters, both those of the ancient observance and those of the reform of St. Teresa of Jesus (d. 1582), have at all times been zealous in spreading far and wide the love of prayer, the desire for evangelical perfection, and devotion to the Mother of Christ.

Their special devotion is to the Blessed Virgin under the title of "Our Lady of Mount Carmel": as they make their journey to the "mountain which is Christ" (Col), she cherishes them as a loving mother, protects them as a sure patroness, and accompanies them as a faithful sister. The Carmelites, though they are assiduous in meditating on the totality of the mystery of the Blessed Virgin Mary, are particularly devoted to contemplation of our Lady intent on prayer, or leading her hidden life, or treasuring the words of the Lord in her heart, or doing her works of charity.

Our Lady has always been known by the Carmelite brothers and sisters as "mother and teacher in the Spirit" because she was a perfect disciple of Christ and "is still a mother, continuing to give [God] children. . . , encouraging them by her love, and drawing them by her example to pursue perfect charity" (Pref).

In this formulary our Lady is celebrated as:

—*a teacher*, who keeps the words of the Lord in her heart (cf. *All*, Com Ant, Luke 2:19, 51), who "instructs by her example" (PO), teaching "fear of the Lord" (Ent Ant, cf. Psalm 34:12); who, since she is "the model of all who live by the spirit of the Gospel" (Pref), teaches us, "as we look up to her in prayer . . . to love [God] above all things," to be "rapt in contemplation" of his Word, and untiringly to "serve the needs of others" (Pref);

—*a mother*, who gently invites us to "go up to the mountain of the Lord" (Ent Ant; cf. Isaiah 2:3), which is Christ himself (cf. Col); a mother through whom Wisdom says: "whoever find me, finds life" (Proverbs 8:35; cf. 1 Read, Proverbs 8:17-21, 34-35); a mother, who accepted us as her children at the foot of the Cross (cf. Gos, John 19:25-27), who "watches over [us] by her patronage" (PO) and keeps us "fortified by her protection" (Col).

With some changes, this Mass is taken from the *Proprium missarum Fratrum Discalceatorum Ordinis b.mae Mariae Virginis de Monte Carmelo*, Curia Generalis OCD, Rome, 1973, pp. 51–52, 90.

Entrance Antiphon Psalm 34:12; Isaiah 2:3

Come to me, children, and listen:
I will teach you the fear of the Lord.
Come, let us go up to the mountain of the Lord,
and we shall walk in his ways.

COLLECT

May the venerable intercession of the glorious Virgin Mary
come to our aid, we pray, O Lord,
so that, fortified by her protection,
we may reach the mountain which is Christ.
Who lives and reigns with you in the unity of the Holy Spirit,
God, for ever and ever.

PRAYER OVER THE OFFERINGS

Lord, we offer these gifts from joyful hearts;
through them sanctify your servants,
whom the Blessed Virgin instructs by her example
and watches over by her patronage,
so that, faithful to our baptismal promises,
we may serve you and our neighbor with sincerity of heart.
Through Christ our Lord.

Preface P 32, page 117.

Communion Antiphon Luke 2:19

Mary treasured all these words,
reflecting on them in her heart.

PRAYER AFTER COMMUNION

Lord God,
you have given us new strength
through the Sacrament
of the Sacred Body and Precious Blood of your Son;
grant that this gift of your love
may be our lasting protection
and inspire us to follow faithfully
in the footsteps of the Blessed Virgin Mary
by imitating her virtues.
Through Christ our Lord.

33. THE BLESSED VIRGIN MARY, MOTHER OF GOOD COUNSEL

Whenever the faithful throughout the world recite the Litany of Loreto, they invoke the Blessed Virgin as Mother of Good Counsel, a title Leo XIII inserted into the Litany in 1903. Largely through the work of the brothers and sisters of the Augustinian family, devotion to the Mother of Good Counsel has spread far and wide from the town of Genazzano, not far from Rome, which has a famous sanctuary dedicated to her.

Our Lady is rightly honored under this title, for she is the Mother of Christ, whom Isaiah with prophetic vision called "Wonderful Counselor" (Isaiah 9:5: cf. 1 Read, Isaiah 9:1-3, 5-6; PC); she lived her whole life under the guidance of the "Spirit of counsel," who "overshadowed" her (PO); she "gave herself wholeheartedly to [God's] wise and loving plan for renewing all things in Christ" (Pref; cf. Ephesians 1:10); "generously [God] poured out" on her "the gifts of [the] Holy Spirit" (Pref), principal among which is the "spirit of wisdom" (Ent Ant, cf. Wisdom 7:7b).

In the texts of this Mass our Lady, enlightened by the gift of counsel, is honored as Mother and teacher as she cries out in gratitude in the words of Wisdom itself: "To me belong counsel and prudence, understanding and strength are mine" (*All*, Proverbs 8:14); gifts willingly shared with the children and disciples of Wisdom (cf. Ent Ant), whom Mary instructs that they must before all else do what Christ has told them to do (cf. Gos, John 2:1-11; Com Ant, John 2:5).

In celebrating this Mass we earnestly ask God for the gift of counsel, to teach us how to know his will and to guide us in all we do (Col; cf. PC).

This Mass, except for the Preface, is taken from the *Proprium missarum Ordinis Fratrum sancti Augustini*, approved in 1975 by the Congregation for Divine Worship.

Entrance Antiphon Wisdom 7:7b, 13

I called upon God,
and there came to me the spirit of wisdom;
I learned wisdom in simplicity of heart,
I hand it on ungrudgingly, I do not hide away its riches.

COLLECT

Lord, you know that our thoughts on earth
are full of fear and uncertainty;
through the intercession of the Blessed Virgin Mary,
from whom your Son took flesh and blood,
send us the gift of counsel
to teach us how to discern your will
and to guide us in all we do.
Through our Lord Jesus Christ, your Son,
who lives and reigns with you in the unity of the Holy Spirit,
God, for ever and ever.

PRAYER OVER THE OFFERINGS

Lord, let the Spirit of counsel,
who so wonderfully overshadowed your handmaid, the Blessed Virgin,
come upon the gifts we present in worship
and make them pleasing to you.
Through Christ our Lord.

Preface P 33, page 118.

Communion Antiphon Cf. John 2:5

The Mother of Jesus said to the servants: Do whatever he tells you.

PRAYER AFTER COMMUNION

Lord our God,
we have shared in your mysteries
on this memorial of our Lady, Mother of Good Counsel.
Grant that we may learn what is pleasing to you
and receive salvation from your Son,
whom you gave us through the Blessed Virgin Mary
to be our Wonderful Counselor.
Through Christ our Lord.

34. THE BLESSED VIRGIN MARY, CAUSE OF OUR JOY

Christ Jesus came into the world to bring peace and joy to the human family (cf. John 15:11; 17:13). At his birth he filled the humble shepherds with joy (cf. Luke 2:10), at his Resurrection he brought joy to the disciples (cf. John 20:20; Luke 24:41), at his Ascension he left the apostles in great joy (cf. Luke 24:52); from his place at the right hand of the Father he sent upon the infant Church the Spirit of love and joy (cf. Galatians 5:22).

The Church as the Bride of Christ has always found joy in its Bridegroom and returned his love with ever-increasing joy. Since Jesus had come to us through Mary, the Church came gradually to understand that the Blessed Virgin, because of her cooperation in the incarnation of the Word, is the cause or origin or source of this great joy; the Church has known too that the sorrow brought into the world by Eve's disobedience has been changed into joy by Mary's obedience, and so it began to honor her with the title "cause of our joy." Devotion to our Lady under this title has developed especially in France and Canada *(Notre Dame de Liesse).*

The texts of this Mass recall the saving actions of God through Christ in the Holy Spirit that have brought joy to the Blessed Virgin or to the Church or to humanity. The texts celebrate in particular:

—*the choice of our Lady,* who from eternity "found favor with God" (Ent Ant, cf. Luke 1:30), and was chosen as God's dwelling place ("See, I am coming to dwell among you" [1 Read, A, Zechariah 2:14]), as "the city of God" made glad by "the streams of a river" (Com Ant, Psalm 46:5); and therefore as the city-bride clothed "with a robe of salvation" and robed "in a mantle of justice" (cf. 1 Read, B, Isaiah 61:10). Hence in the Mass resound joyful voices: "Rejoice, Virgin Mary" (Ent Ant, cf. Luke 1:28); "Sing and rejoice, O daughter Zion" (1 Read, A, Zechariah 2:14); "Hail, . . . joy of humankind" (*All*);

—*the birth of the Virgin,* which "heralded joy for all the world" (Pref);

—*the visit of Mary to Elizabeth,* when our Lady spoke her canticle of joy and jubilation (cf. Resp, Luke 1:46-48, 49-50, 53-54) and the infant John leapt in his mother's womb because of the coming of the Savior (cf. Gos, Luke 1:39-47);

—*the birth of our Lord,* for God was pleased to bring "joy to the world through the Incarnation of [his] Son" (Col); the motherhood of the Virgin "brought forth [to us] the true Light" (Pref), and also "salvation and joy" (*All*);

—*the Resurrection of Christ:* for we pray to God that we may be guided to eternal happiness "through the saving power of [Christ's] Resurrection" (PC);

—*the Assumption of our Lady:* for "her passing into glory raised her to the heights of heaven, where . . . she waits for us with loving care until we too enjoy the vision of [God's] glory for ever" (Pref).

Entrance Antiphon Cf. Luke 1:28, 30-31

**Rejoice, Virgin Mary, you have found favor with God!
Listen; you will conceive and bear a son,
and you shall call his name Jesus.**

COLLECT

**Lord our God, you were pleased to bring joy to the world
through the Incarnation of your Son.
Grant that we who honor his Mother,
the cause of our joy,
may always walk in the way of your commandments
with our hearts set on true and lasting joy.
Through our Lord Jesus Christ, your Son,
who lives and reigns with you in the unity of the Holy Spirit,
God, for ever and ever.**

PRAYER OVER THE OFFERINGS

**Lord, receive the offerings of your joyful Church,
and as you have given us every good gift
in Christ the Savior,
born of the immaculate Virgin,
grant us a share in his harvest of everlasting joy.
Through Christ our Lord.**

Preface P 34, page 119.

Communion Antiphon

A **The streams of a river make glad the city of God,** Psalm 46:5
the holy dwelling-place of the Most High.

B **All generations will call me blessed,** Lk 1: 48-49
for he who is mighty has done great things for me,
and holy is his name.

PRAYER AFTER COMMUNION

Confirm in our minds the mysteries of the true faith,
we pray, O Lord,
so that, confessing that he who was conceived of the
Virgin Mary,
is true God and true man,
we may, through the saving power of his Resurrection,
merit to attain eternal joy.
Through Christ our Lord.

35. THE BLESSED VIRGIN MARY, PILLAR OF FAITH

The Blessed Virgin is a woman of outstanding faith, a disciple who in a certain sense sums up and re-echoes in her own person the main themes of Christian teaching (cf. LG, no. 65), a mother supporting and protecting the faith of her children.

—*A woman of outstanding faith:* Elizabeth, the mother of the Precursor, called her blessed for her belief in God's message (cf. Luke 1:45); she conceived God's Son in faith and, supported by faith, she followed Jesus and stood beside the Cross, enduring the sight of his Death; in faith she believed that he would rise again, and waited for the coming of the Spirit, promised by the Father.

—*A disciple summing up in her own person the teachings of the faith:* our Lady, as the Second Vatican Council proclaims, "was intimately involved in the history of salvation, and in a certain sense unites and reflects in her own person the chief teachings of the faith" (LG, no. 65); her Immaculate Conception shows the freedom and munificence of God in choosing the instruments of salvation and grace; her consent to the work of salvation in the Incarnation proclaims the meaning and power of human cooperation in God's saving plan; the virginal birth of Christ shows that he is truly God and truly human; her holiness and her state of life—as virgin, wife, and mother—sketch out the features of the Church; her Assumption prefigures the future glory of the human race.

—*A mother supporting the faith of her children:* our Lady, gloriously reigning in heaven, works in a mysterious way on earth, as she points out to her children the way of truth. It has often happened that where love and devotion toward Mary were strong the people have kept the faith even though they were deprived of all spiritual help.

The glorious Mother of God, who destroys all heresies, who undoes the power of error and exposes the falsehood of idols (cf. the Hymn *Akathistos*, vv. 111–112; ed. G. G. Meersseman, *Der Hymnos Akathistos im Abendland*, vol. 1, Universitätsverlag, Freiburg, Switzerland, 1958, p. 114), has in consequence been invoked by the Christian people from very early times as a "pillar of faith."

This Mass, in which we ask that we may be "steadfast in faith" (PO) and "strong in faith" (Col) and "true to the faith on earth" (PC), reproduces in great part the Mass of "Nuestra Señora del Pilar" (cf. *Misal Romano reformado por mandato del Concilio Vaticano II . . ., editio typica* approved by the Episcopal Conference of Spain, Coeditores Liturgicos, Madrid, 1978, pp. 659–660).

Entrance Antiphon Cf. Wisdom 18:3; Exodus 13:21-22

A Mary, Virgin Mother, you are like the pillar of light that,
day and night, went before God's people
to direct their footsteps through the wilderness.

B Mother of Christ, queen of glory, you conceived your Son in faith
and believed that after dying for us he would rise again;
you show yourself a loving mother to the Church
and a pillar of its faith.

COLLECT

Almighty and eternal God,
you gave the Blessed Virgin Mary,
glorious Mother of your Son,
as a pillar of strength
to all who call upon her aid;
grant through her intercession
that we may be strong in faith,
unwavering in hope, and steadfast in love.
Through our Lord Jesus Christ, your Son,
who lives and reigns with you in the unity of the Holy Spirit,
God, for ever and ever.

PRAYER OVER THE OFFERINGS

Lord, all-holy Father,
you have enlightened our minds
with the light of faith;
grant that, through the intercession
of the loving Mother of the Redeemer,
our offerings and prayers
may keep us steadfast in faith
and untiring in love.
Through Christ our Lord.

Preface P 35, page 120.

Communion Antiphon Luke 1:48

From this day all generations will call me blessed:
the Almighty has done great things for me.

PRAYER AFTER COMMUNION

Lord our God,
present in your Church in many ways,
we thank you for the Sacrament we have received
and pray that, with the support of the Blessed Virgin Mary,
we may be true to the faith on earth
and so enjoy the vision of your glory in heaven.
Through Christ our Lord.

36. THE BLESSED VIRGIN MARY, MOTHER OF FAIREST LOVE

In the *Missale Romanum* (1962), there is a Mass of Blessed Mary, Queen of Saints and Mother of Fairest Love, in the section, *Pro aliquibis locis* (for certain places), celebrated on 8 May (earlier on 31 May).

The expression "mother of fairest love" is found in the Vulgate text of Sirach 24:24 ("I am the mother of fairest love, of reverence, of knowledge, and of holy hope"): from the tenth century it has been frequently used in Masses of our Lady.

In this Mass the Church, following tradition of both East and West, as it celebrates the mystery and role of our Lady, contemplates with joy her spiritual beauty. Beauty is the radiance of the holiness and truth of God, "the origin of all beauty" (cf. Col, B), and it is the image of the goodness and fidelity of Christ, "fairest of all [God's] children on earth" (Col, A; Psalm 45:3).

In this formulary the Blessed Virgin is called "beautiful" for three reasons: because as "full of grace" (Gos, Luke 1:28) and "adorned with the gifts of the Holy Spirit" (Col, C), she "is resplendent . . . with the glory of her Son and the beauty of holiness" (Col, B); because she loved God, her Son, in all his radiance, and all members of the human race, with a love that was full of beauty, that is, with a love that was virginal, bridal, and maternal; because she shared so beautifully in the mystery of the conception and birth of Christ and his Death and Resurrection (cf. Pref), that is, she shared in God's saving plan with courage and gentleness, with cooperation and fidelity.

To celebrate our Lady's spiritual beauty, the formulary makes use of biblical and patristic figures and images customary in the liturgy. In our Lady, who is "all fair" and in whom there is "no flaw" (cf. Resp, Song of Songs 4:7), are found in the highest degree the celebrated virtues of the women of the Old Testament: the beauty and love of the bride in the Song of Songs (cf. Ent Ant, B, Song of Songs 6:10; Resp); the beauty and wisdom of Judith (cf. Com Ant, B, Judith 11:21); the splendor and grace of the Queen, the Bride of the messianic King (cf. Com Ant, B, Psalm 45:3).

The "way of beauty" is the way of Christian perfection: the faithful, as they walk "with the Blessed Virgin" (cf. PO), strive to "walk always in the ways of [God's] justice" (PC) and ask God that they may "turn away from the ugliness of sin and love only the beauty that comes from [the] Spirit" (Col, C).

Entrance Antiphon

A Go forth, daughters of Zion,
and see your queen; the morning stars sing her praises,
sun and moon bow before her beauty,
and all God's children rejoice in her presence.

B Daughter of Zion, full of loveliness and grace, Cf. Song of Songs 6:10; Luke 1:42
you are fair as the moon,
glorious as the sun, most favored of all women.

COLLECT

A Lord our God, by the wonder of your wisdom
Jesus Christ, the Bridegroom of the Church
and fairest of all your children on earth,
came forth from a virgin's womb;
through the intercession of his Mother in her glory
give joy and peace to all peoples
and fill our hearts with the light of your holiness.
Through our Lord Jesus Christ, your Son,
who lives and reigns with you in the unity of the Holy Spirit,
God, for ever and ever.

B Lord God,
your lowly handmaid, the Virgin Mary,
is resplendent in your presence
with the glory of her Son and the beauty of holiness;
grant that like her
we may seek only what is true and just
and so come before you, the origin of all beauty
and the author of purest love.
Through our Lord Jesus Christ, your Son,
who lives and reigns with you in the unity of the Holy Spirit,
God, for ever and ever.

C Lord,
let the Virgin Mary in her glory intercede for us;
adorned with the gifts of the Holy Spirit,
she won your favor
and brought forth for us your only Son,
fair beyond all your children on earth.
Grant that we may turn away from the ugliness of sin
and love only the beauty that comes from your Spirit.
Through our Lord Jesus Christ, your Son,
who lives and reigns with you in the unity of the Holy Spirit,
God, for ever and ever.

PRAYER OVER THE OFFERINGS

May we receive, O Lord, we pray,
the effects of this offering dedicated to you,
so that, walking with the Blessed Virgin Mary in the way
of beauty,
we may be renewed by growth in heavenly life
and come at last to the vision of your glory.
Through Christ our Lord.

Preface P 36, page 122.

Communion Antiphon

A No other woman can compare with her, Cf. Judith 11:21
in the beauty of her face, in the wisdom of her words.

B Graciousness is poured out upon your lips, Psalm 45:3
for God has blessed you for ever more.

PRAYER AFTER COMMUNION

Lord God,
continue to bless with your unending favor
those whom you renew in strength by this holy Sacrament;
and let those to whom you have presented the Blessed
Virgin Mary
in all the beauty of her virtue
walk always in the ways of your justice.
Through Christ our Lord.

37. THE BLESSED VIRGIN MARY, MOTHER OF DIVINE HOPE

The Second Vatican Council at the end of its Dogmatic Constitution on the Church *Lumen gentium* says of the Blessed Virgin that she "shines upon our world, until the day of the Lord shall come (cf. 2 Peter 3:10), as a sign of sure hope and comfort for your people on their pilgrim way" (no. 68). These words are found almost verbatim in the Preface of the Mass of the Assumption (cf. *The Roman Missal*, Pref for the Assumption, 15 August).

In considering our Lady's role in the history of salvation, the Church often refers to her as "our hope" (Final Marian Ant, *Salve, Regina*, "Hail, holy Queen"; hymn at Morning Prayer, 8 December, LH, 1972) and as "Mother of hope" (cf. hymn at Office of Readings, 21 November, LH, 1972; cf. the Vulgate text of Sirach 24:24); on the birthday of our Lady the Church rejoices because she brought "the daybreak of hope and salvation for all the world" (PC, 8 September); recalling her role as mother in the process of salvation, the Church sings in petition: "O gate of everlasting life, / With loving heart our prayer receive: / Through you our hope of life was born, / When hope was lost through sin of Eve" (English translation of hymn at Evening Prayer, 22 August, LH, 1972); in the mystery of our Lady's glorious Assumption the Church looks on Mary as "the sure hope of salvation," shining on all the faithful "through life's sharp thorns" (hymn at Morning Prayer, 15 August, LH, 1972). On 9 July in some particular Churches there is a liturgical celebration of the Blessed Virgin Mary, Mother of Divine Hope, and notably in the Congregation of the Passion of Jesus Christ (Passionists), from whose *Proprium Missarum*, Curia Generalis CP, Rome, 1974, pp. 21–22, several texts of this formulary are taken.

In this Mass the Mother of Christ is venerated:

—because in her life on earth she constantly practiced the virtue of hope; "she placed all her trust" in the Lord (Pref), "she awaited in hope and conceived in faith the Son of Man, whom the prophets had foretold" (Pref);

—because in her Assumption into heaven she became the "hope of God's people" (Ent Ant); for she comes "to the aid of all who have no hope" (Ent Ant) and looks with love on all who seek her help, giving them strength and comfort (cf. Col, A, Col, B, Ent Ant);

—because she is a "beacon of unfailing hope" and solace (Col, B) for "all the children of Adam" (Pref) "until the day of the Lord dawns in glory" (Pref).

Entrance Antiphon

Hail, Virgin Mary, hope of God's people:
you come to the aid of all who have no hope,
you look with love on all who seek your help.

COLLECT

A Lord our God, you give us the joy
of honoring the Blessed Virgin Mary
as Mother of divine hope.
In your mercy
grant that, through her prayers and help,
we may always live as good citizens of this world,
with our hearts fixed on the world to come,
and so receive what we look forward to in faith,
the fulfillment of all our hope.
Through our Lord Jesus Christ, your Son,
who lives and reigns with you in the unity of the Holy Spirit,
God, for ever and ever.

B Lord God,
you have given the Blessed Virgin Mary to your Church
as a beacon of unfailing hope.
In your goodness
grant that those who are burdened by life's cares
may find in her consolation and strength
and those who despair of salvation
may find their hearts warmed and uplifted
as they turn to her in their need.
Through our Lord Jesus Christ, your Son,
who lives and reigns with you in the unity of the Holy Spirit,
God, for ever and ever.

PRAYER OVER THE OFFERINGS

Receive, O Lord, we ask, the prayers of your people
with the sacrificial offerings,
that, through the intercession of Blessed Mary,
the Mother of your Son,
no petition may go unanswered,
no request be made in vain.
Through Christ our Lord.

Preface P 37, page 124.

Communion Antiphon

A **Blessed are you who have believed** Luke 1:45
that what was spoken to you by the Lord will be fulfilled.

B **Let us live justly and devoutly in this age,** Titus 2:12-13
as we await blessed hope
and the coming of the glory of our great God
and of our Savior, Jesus Christ.

PRAYER AFTER COMMUNION

Having received the Sacrament
of salvation and faith,
we humbly beseech you, O Lord,
that we, who honor the Blessed Virgin, Mother of our hope,
may be worthy to share with her
in the charity of heaven.
Through Christ our Lord.

38. HOLY MARY, MOTHER OF UNITY

The example of Christ as he prayed to the Father that "they may all be one" (Gos, A, John 17:21) is an encouragement to all his disciples to be earnest themselves in their prayers for Christian unity.

The Catholic Church, in its zeal for the unity of Christians, and indeed of the whole human family, asks God that, through the intercession of the Blessed Virgin, "all the families of nations . . . may be gathered together to form the one people of the New Covenant" (Col). For the Church is convinced that the cause of Christian unity rightly belongs to the spiritual motherhood of the Blessed Virgin Mary (cf. Leo XIII, Encyclical Letter *Adiutricem populi*, AAS 28 [1895–1896], p. 135). Hence Paul VI referred more than once to the Blessed Virgin as "Mother of unity" (cf. *Insegnamenti di Paolo VI*, III, p. 69).

The formulary of this Mass first of all celebrates God as "fountain of unity and wellspring of harmony" (Col); then it recalls the one Mediator between God and the human race, Jesus Christ (cf. 1 Read, 1 Timothy 2:5), who, the day before he suffered, prayed to the Father for the disciples that they might be made perfect in unity (cf. Gos, B, John 17:20-26); it also commemorates the Blessed Virgin, who played an important role in the history of salvation with reference to the "mystery of unity":

—*in the mystery of the Incarnation*, when in her "virginal womb" the Word of God "united divine and human nature" in an unbreakable bond (PO);

—*in her virginal motherhood*, when the Son of God "chose for his Mother a woman unstained in heart and body" (Pref), who would be the image of "his Bride, the one and undivided Church" (Pref);

—*in the Passion of Christ*, when Jesus, "lifted high above the earth, in the presence of his Mother . . . gathered [God's] scattered children into unity" (Pref);

—*in the outpouring of the Holy Spirit*, when Jesus, returning to the Father, "sent upon the Blessed Virgin, at prayer with the Apostles, the Spirit of concord and unity, of peace and forgiveness" (Pref; cf. Ent Ant, B).

Entrance Antiphon

A Rejoice and be glad, Virgin Mary, for all God's children will be reunited and will bless the everlasting Lord. Cf. Tobit 13:13

B The disciples devoted themselves with one accord to prayer with Mary, the Mother of Jesus. Cf. Acts 1:14

COLLECT

All-holy Father,
fountain of unity and wellspring of harmony,
grant that all the families of nations,
through the intercession of the Blessed Virgin Mary,
Mother of the human race,
may be gathered together
to form the one people of the New Covenant.
Through our Lord Jesus Christ, your Son,
who lives and reigns with you in the unity of the Holy Spirit,
God, for ever and ever.

PRAYER OVER THE OFFERINGS

Lord,
as we honor the memory of the Blessed Virgin Mary,
in whose virginal womb
your Son united divine and human nature,
we earnestly beg
that this offering may become
the Sacrament of our worship,
the sign of our unity,
and the bond of our love.
Through Christ our Lord.

Preface P 38, page 125.

Communion Antiphon Cf. 1 Corinthians 10:17

Though man, we are one bread, one body,
for we all partake of the one Bread and one Chalice.

PRAYER AFTER COMMUNION

Lord God, through your holy gifts
which we have received
on this memorial of holy Mary, Mother of unity,
pour out upon us
the Spirit of gentleness and peace,
that we may work together in harmony
and so hasten the coming of your Kingdom.
Through Christ our Lord.

SECTION 3

This section contains eight Mass formularies for the celebration of a memorial of Mary under titles that refer to her merciful intercession on behalf of the faithful.

MASS FORMULARIES

39. HOLY MARY, QUEEN AND MOTHER OF MERCY

The title of this formulary comprises two titles frequently attributed to the Blessed Virgin, both of which speak of her graciousness and are much loved by the faithful: "Queen of mercy" and "Mother of mercy."

The title "Queen of mercy" (Ent Ant, Col, B, *All*) celebrates the kindness, the generosity, the dignity of the Blessed Virgin, who from her place in heaven fulfills the role of Queen Esther (cf. 1 Read, Esther 4:17), "never ceasing to pray" to her Son (Pref) for the salvation of her people as they confidently fly to her for refuge in their trials and dangers. The Blessed Virgin is thus the "gracious" and "compassionate" queen (Pref, PC) "who has herself uniquely known [God's] loving kindness and stretches out her arms to embrace all who take refuge in her" (Pref; cf. PC); hence she is rightly addressed as "solace of the repentant, hope of the distressed" (Ent Ant).

The title "Mother of mercy" (Col, A, Pref, PO) is thought to have been first given to the Blessed Virgin by St. Odo (d. 942), Abbot of Cluny (cf. *Vita Odonis* I:9: PL 133:47). It is a fitting title of our Lady both because she brought forth for us Jesus Christ, the visible manifestation of the mercy of the invisible God, and because she is the spiritual mother of the faithful, full of grace and mercy; in the words of St. Lawrence of Brindisi, "the Blessed Virgin is called 'mother of mercy,' that is, the most merciful, the most compassionate mother, the most tender mother, the most loving mother" (*Mariale*, Second sermon on the "Salve Regina," III: *Opera omnia*, I, Seminary Press, Padua, 1928, p. 391). For the Mother of Jesus from her place in heaven points out the needs of the faithful to her Son, with whom she interceded on earth on behalf of the bridegroom and bride of Cana (cf. Gos, John 2:1-11).

In this formulary the Blessed Virgin is celebrated as:

—*a prophet extolling the mercy of God* (cf. Gos, Luke 1:39-55): for in her Magnificat she twice praises God's mercy: "He has mercy on those who fear him in every generation"; "He has come to the help of his servant Israel, for he has remembered his promise of mercy" (Luke 1:50, 54; cf. Com Ant, B). The faithful therefore pray that they "may always praise [God's] mercy in company with the Blessed Virgin" (PC);

—*a woman who has uniquely experienced God's mercy:* "She is the gracious queen who has herself uniquely known [God's] loving kindness and stretches out her arms to embrace all who . . . call upon her help in their distress" (Pref). These words of the Preface echo those of Pope John Paul II: "Mary is . . . the one who obtained mercy in a particular and exceptional way, as no other person has . . ." (Encyclical Letter *Dives in misericordia*, no. 9: AAS 72 [1980], pp. 1208–1209).

Entrance Antiphon

**Hail, Queen of mercy, Mother of Christ in your glory,
solace of the repentant, hope of the distressed.**

COLLECT

A **God, whose mercy is without measure,
through the prayers of the Blessed Virgin Mary,
Mother of mercy,
grant that we may know your loving kindness on earth
and come at last to the glory of heaven.
Through our Lord Jesus Christ, your Son,
who lives and reigns with you in the unity of the Holy Spirit,
God, for ever and ever.**

B **All-holy Father,
hear the prayers of your children,
weighed down by our sinfulness,
as we turn to you and call upon the merciful love
that moved you to send your Son as Savior of the world
and to enthrone holy Mary as the Queen of mercy.
Through our Lord Jesus Christ, your Son,
who lives and reigns with you in the unity of the Holy Spirit,
God, for ever and ever.**

PRAYER OVER THE OFFERINGS

**Lord, receive the gifts of your people,
and grant that as we look up
to the Blessed Virgin, Mother of mercy,
we may show ourselves merciful to others
and receive your pardon toward us.
Through Christ our Lord.**

Preface P 39, page 126.

Communion Antiphon

A Be merciful as your Father is merciful. Luke 6:36

B The Almighty has done great things for me, Luke 1:49-50
and holy is his Name.
He has mercy on those who fear him
in every generation.

PRAYER AFTER COMMUNION

Lord God,
you have given us food and drink from heaven;
grant that we may always praise your mercy
in company with the Blessed Virgin
and rejoice in her protection,
for we acknowledge her as our queen,
compassionate to sinners
and merciful to the poor.
Through Christ our Lord.

40. THE BLESSED VIRGIN MARY, MOTHER OF DIVINE PROVIDENCE

In 1744 Benedict XIV (d. 1758) granted to the Congregation of Clerks Regular of St. Paul (Barnabites) a Mass in honor of the Blessed Virgin Mary, "Mother of Divine Providence," venerated at Rome in the church of St. Charles, known popularly as "ai Catinari." This Mass was to be celebrated on the Saturday before the third Sunday of November. Several other religious institutes also observe this memorial.

This title celebrates the role entrusted by God, whose "loving providence is always wise and unfailing" (Col), to the Blessed Virgin as:

—*the loving Mother of Christ* (PO), for "in the wisdom of [God's] providence the Blessed Virgin Mary . . . gave birth to the Savior of the world" (Pref);

—*a mother who cares for each of her children* (Pref), "entrusted to her by Christ Jesus while he hung upon the Cross" (Pref);

—*the handmaid of God's love* (cf. Pref), for as she interceded with her Son at Cana of Galilee for the bridegroom and the bride (cf. Gos, John 2:1-11; cf. Pref), "now, enthroned as queen at her Son's right hand, she provides for all the needs of the Church" (Pref).

The Blessed Virgin is thus called "Mother of Divine Providence" because she has been given to us by God in his great providence as a generous mother providing us through her intercession with gifts from heaven. Like God, who cannot forget his people (cf. Ent Ant, Isaiah 49:15), indeed consoles them like a mother, so the Blessed Virgin has pity on us (cf. Ent Ant), intercedes for us (cf. Col, PO, PC), comes to the help of the Church in its needs (cf. Pref), and fills us with consolation (cf. 1 Read, Isaiah 66:10-14).

Hence the faithful, relying on the patronage of so great a mother, receive "mercy and grace in [their] time of need" (PO; cf. Hebrews 4:16), and, as in obedience to God's command they "seek . . . above all else" God's Kingdom and its justice, they "receive [God's] help for [their] earthly needs" (PC, cf. Matthew 6:33).

In great part the texts of this Mass are taken from the *Missae Propriae*, Curia Generalis Clericorum Regularium sancti Pauli, Rome, 1981, pp. 60–76.

Entrance Antiphon Isaiah 49:15

Can a mother forget her infant, and not have pity on the child of her womb? Even if a mother should forget, you I will never forget.

COLLECT

Lord our God,
your loving providence is always wise and unfailing;
through the prayers of the Blessed Virgin,
Mother of your Son,
remove from us all that would harm us
and grant us all that will be for our good.
Through our Lord Jesus Christ, your Son,
who lives and reigns with you in the unity of the Holy Spirit,
God, for ever and ever.

PRAYER OVER THE OFFERINGS

Lord, in your goodness
accept the gifts of your Church,
so that, through the loving intercession
of the Mother of your Son,
we may receive your mercy and grace
in our time of need.
Through Christ our Lord.

Preface P 40, page 127.

Communion Antiphon Cf. Psalm 87:3; Luke 1:49

**Glorious things are spoken of you, O Virgin Mary,
for he who is mighty has done great things for you.**

PRAYER AFTER COMMUNION

**God of mercy,
let this heavenly table
continue to strengthen your faithful people,
so that, through the intercession of the Mother of divine providence,
we may seek your Kingdom and its justice
above all else
and receive your help for our earthly needs.
Through Christ our Lord.**

41. THE BLESSED VIRGIN MARY, MOTHER OF CONSOLATION

The actions of the all-powerful and merciful God in coming to the aid of his oppressed or exiled people are described in Scripture as "God's consolation." The supreme consolation is Christ, sent by the Father into the world when the fullness of time had come, to heal the brokenhearted (cf. 1 Read, Isaiah 61:1-3, 10-11).

The Blessed Virgin Mary is herself rightly named and venerated as "Mother of consolation" or "comforter of the afflicted." Through her God "graciously sent Jesus Christ to be the consolation" of his people (Col).

Because she stood beside Christ suffering on the Cross and endured her bitter agony, she gained in the highest degree the blessedness promised in the Gospel to those who mourn (cf. Gos, A, Matthew 5:5); because the Lord consoled her by the Resurrection of Jesus, she in her turn is able to console her children in all their afflictions (cf. Ent Ant, 2 Corinthians 1:3-5).

After the Ascension of Christ, "in company with the Apostles she earnestly prayed and awaited with trust the coming of the Spirit of consolation and peace" (Pref, cf. Gos, B, John 14:15-21, 25-27).

Even now after her Assumption into heaven, she continues to intercede with a mother's love for those in distress. In the Dogmatic Constitution on the Church *Lumen gentium* of the Second Vatican Council we read: "The Mother of Jesus . . . shines forth as a sign of sure hope and consolation for the pilgrim people of God" (no. 68).

The Mother of the Lord is honored in many places under the title of "Mother of consolation" or "comforter of the afflicted," and especially in Turin (on 20 June), where a well-known shrine is dedicated in her honor, and in a large number of religious families, and particularly in the Order of St. Augustine and the Consolata Missionary Institute (Consolata Missionaries), founded by the Servant of God Joseph Allamano (d. 1926).

Entrance Antiphon Cf. 2 Corinthians 1:3

Blessed be God, the Father of mercies and God of all comfort,
who consoles us in all our afflictions.

COLLECT

Lord our God,
through the Virgin Mary
you graciously sent Jesus Christ
to be the consolation of your people;
grant that, through her intercession,
we may be filled with all consolation
and share it among our brothers and sisters.
Through our Lord Jesus Christ, your Son,
who lives and reigns with you in the unity of the Holy Spirit,
God, for ever and ever.

PRAYER OVER THE OFFERINGS

Receive, holy Father, this offering of our humility,
which we bring you with joy
on this memorial of the Blessed Virgin Mary,
and grant, we pray, that it may be for us,
who are joined to the sacrifice of Christ,
our consolation on earth and our eternal salvation.
Through Christ our Lord.

Preface P 41, page 128.

Communion Antiphon Cf. Psalm 87:3, 7

**Glorious things are spoken of you, Virgin Mary;
in you all rejoice to find their home.**

PRAYER AFTER COMMUNION

**Renewed by this Paschal Sacrament,
we pray, O Lord,
that we, who honor the memory of the Mother of your Son
experiencing each day the mystery of death in our bodies,
may be uplifted by hope from heaven
and show forth in our daily lives
the Good News of the Resurrection.
Through Christ our Lord.**

42. THE BLESSED VIRGIN MARY, HELP OF CHRISTIANS

The Church has often experienced the extraordinary help of the Mother of God in times of persecution by the enemies of the Christian faith. Therefore, from the earliest centuries of the Christian era, the custom developed of invoking the Blessed Virgin in the storms of persecution under the title of "help of Christians."

While Pius VII (d. 1823) was held a prisoner after being driven from the See of Peter by force of arms, and the whole Church was praying earnestly to God on his behalf through the intercession of the Blessed Virgin, the Supreme Pontiff was unexpectedly released and, on returning to Rome, was restored to the papal throne on 24 May 1814.

As a result Pius VII established a feast in honor of the Virgin Mother under the title of "help of Christians," to be celebrated at Rome in perpetuity on 24 May, the anniversary of his safe return to the city of Rome. This feast is celebrated in many particular Churches and religious institutes, especially in the Society of St. Francis de Sales (Salesians), founded by St. John Bosco (d. 1888).

The First Reading of this Mass recalls the great conflict established by God's providence between the woman and the serpent from the beginning of the human race. There is a choice of readings:

—either Genesis 3:1-6, 13-15, recounting God's threatening words to the serpent and the first proclamation of the future victory of the Son of the woman: "I will put enmity between you and the woman, and between your offspring and hers; he will strike at your head, while you strike at his heel" (v. 15);

—or Revelation 12:1-3a, 7-12ab, 17, which prophetically narrates the warfare of the great dragon or ancient serpent (cf. vv. 3, 9) against the woman clothed with the sun and crowned with twelve stars (cf. v. 1), and against the rest "of her offspring, those who keep God's commandments and bear witness to Jesus" (v. 17); that is, against the Church, represented under the image of the Virgin Mary.

The Gospel reading (John 2:1-11) calls to mind the help that, by nourishing the faith of Christians and responding to their needs, the Blessed Virgin continuously bestows on the Church—symbolized by the disciples who believe in Jesus (cf. v. 11) and the guests at the wedding feast (cf. v. 2).

The euchological texts of the Mass celebrate the action of God in appointing the Blessed Virgin, "Mother of [his] beloved Son" (Col), "Mother and help of Christians" (Col, Pref), "so that under her protection we might be fearless in waging the battle of faith, steadfast in holding the teaching of the Apostles, and tranquil in spirit in the storms of this world" (Pref; cf. Col, PO).

The texts of this Mass, except for the Preface, are taken, with some changes, from the *Propria missarum* of the Society of St. Francis de Sales (Vatican Polyglot Press, 1974, pp. 35–40) and that of the Congregation of Clerks Regular of St. Paul (Curia Generalis, Rome, 1981, pp. 25–29).

Entrance Antiphon — Cf. Judith 13:19

People will never cease to praise you,
as they recall the power of the Lord for ever.

COLLECT

Lord our God,
you chose the Mother of your beloved Son
to be the Mother and help of Christians;
grant that we may live under her protection
and that your Church may enjoy unbroken peace.
Through our Lord Jesus Christ, your Son,
who lives and reigns with you in the unity of the Holy Spirit,
God, for ever and ever.

PRAYER OVER THE OFFERINGS

Lord, we offer you this sacrifice of praise
as we rejoice in this memorial of the Mother of your Son;
grant that through the help of so great a mother
we may find you coming to our rescue in every trial.
Through Christ our Lord.

Preface P 42, page 130.

Communion Antiphon — Deuteronomy 10:21a

The Lord, who has done great things for you,
is your praise and your God.

PRAYER AFTER COMMUNION

Lord God, refreshed by this heavenly Sacrament
and relying on the help of the Blessed Virgin Mary,
we ask that we may cast aside the old ways of sin
and put on Jesus Christ,
the author of the new creation.
Who lives and reigns for ever and ever.

43. OUR LADY OF RANSOM

Among the religious families dedicated by a special bond to the Mother of Christ is the Order of Our Lady of Ransom, founded for the ransom of Christian captives by St. Peter Nolasco (d. 1256) in Barcelona in 1218, after consultation with St. Raymond of Penyafort (d. 1275) and King James I of Aragon (d. 1276).

Our Lady of Ransom is essentially venerated in Aragon and Catalonia and in many regions of Latin America.

This formulary, in view of the purpose for which the Order (the Mercedarians) was founded, is primarily a celebration of Christ as "Redeemer of the human race" (Col), who merited by his sacrifice "the true liberty of [God's] children" (Col).

It is also a commemoration of our Lady, who is rightly called "the handmaid of our redemption" (Pref) because she is the handmaid of the Lord (cf. Luke 1:38), totally dedicated to the work of her Son, the Redeemer (cf. LG, no. 56).

In this Mass our Lady is celebrated as:

—*a new Judith:* just as the first Judith courageously freed her people from the siege by Holofernes, so Mary in her warfare against the serpent, the ancient enemy, brought blessings on the people of Israel and on the whole Church (cf. 1 Read, Judith 15:8-10; 16:13-14);

—*the prophetess of the redemption of Israel:* becoming the voice of her people, she magnified the Lord, because, mindful of his mercy, he had come to the rescue of Israel by redeeming it from slavery to sin (cf. Ent Ant, Luke 1:46a, 54-55a);

—*the companion in the Passion of Christ:* our Lady was a loving mother of her Son "in his infancy" and stood at the foot of his Cross "as the faithful companion in his Passion" (Pref); the Gospel reading is appropriately taken from the passage in John recording her presence beside the Cross (Gos, John 19:25-27);

—*a loving mother,* given to us by God in his mercy (cf. PC), one who "cares unceasingly with a mother's love for all [God's] children in their need, breaking the chains of every form of captivity, that [we] might enjoy full liberty of body and spirit" (Pref);

—*"our advocate"* (Pref) and *"patroness in heaven"* (PC): Mary, "assumed into heaven" (Pref), is always interceding for us.

The texts of this Mass are taken from the *Proprium missarum Ordinis beatae Mariae Virginis de Mercede*, Curia Generalis Ordinis, Rome, 1976, pp. 26–28 and 50.

Entrance Antiphon Luke 1:46a, 54-55a

My soul proclaims the greatness of the Lord.
He has come to the help of his servant Israel,
for he has remembered his promise of mercy,
the promise made to our ancestors.

COLLECT

God, the Father of mercies,
you sent your Son into the world
as Redeemer of the human race;
grant that we who honor his Mother as Our Lady of Ransom
may faithfully protect
and seek to spread to all peoples
the true liberty of your children,
which Christ the Lord merited by his sacrifice.
Who lives and reigns with you in the unity of the Holy Spirit,
God, for ever and ever.

PRAYER OVER THE OFFERINGS

Receive, O Lord, the offerings of our devotion,
and grant that we, who celebrate
your Son's work of boundless charity,
may, through the example of the Blessed Virgin Mary,
be confirmed in love of you and of our neighbor.
Through Christ our Lord.

Preface P 43, page 130.

Communion Antiphon John 2:5

The Mother of Jesus said to the attendants: Do whatever he tells you.

PRAYER AFTER COMMUNION

Lord God,
we have received the Sacrament of redemption and life
and now pray that through the intercession of Our Lady
of Ransom,
whom in your mercy you gave us
as our loving Mother and patroness in heaven,
we may serve ever more strenuously
the mystery of salvation on earth
and be at last admitted into your heavenly Kingdom.
Through Christ our Lord.

44. THE BLESSED VIRGIN MARY, HEALTH OF THE SICK

Divine healing affects our whole human nature, body, soul, and spirit, while we are pilgrims here on earth and especially citizens of heaven. Through the healing made possible by Christ in the Holy Spirit, our human condition is completely altered: oppression is changed into liberty, ignorance into knowledge of the truth, sickness into health, affliction into joy, death into life, slavery to sin into a share in the divine nature. Yet we cannot achieve absolute and perfect healing in this world: our life is exposed to suffering, illness, and death. But "God's healing" is Jesus Christ himself, whom the Father sent into the world as our Savior and as the physician of body and soul, as the liturgy describes him, echoing the words of St. Ignatius of Antioch (cf. *Ad Ephesios*, VII, 2: Sch, 10, p. 74). In the days of his flesh, moved by compassion, he healed many sick people, often freeing them at the same time from the wound of sin.

Our Lady also, as the Mother of Christ, our Savior, and Mother of the faithful, with heartfelt love comes to the help of her children in their troubles. That is why sick people flock to her in great numbers, often going to shrines dedicated to her, so that they may be healed through her intercession. In these Marian shrines there are many testimonies to the confidence that sick people have in the Mother of Christ.

Among the titles under which the Blessed Virgin is venerated by the sick that of "health of the sick" is preeminent. It was made popular especially through the zeal of the members of the Order of Clerks Regular, Ministers to the Sick, whose church of St. Mary Magdalene in Rome possesses a Marian image celebrated for its veneration by the faithful and the miracles associated with it.

In the Liturgy of the Word one of Isaiah's Songs of the Servant is read (1 Read, Isaiah 53:1-5, 7-10): "it was our pain that he bore, our sufferings he endured" (v. 4), "by his wounds we were healed" (v. 5). The congregation responds by blessing God, "who heals every one of your ills" (Resp, Psalm 103:1a, 3b).

The Gospel reading is from St. Luke's account of the visitation (Gos, Luke 1:39-56), so that the faithful, as they see our Lady, full of faith and praising God's loving kindness, hastening to visit the mother of the Precursor, may be inspired to show the same loving care to their sick brothers and sisters.

In the Liturgy of the Eucharist God the Father is glorified for giving to the sick a patroness and model in our Lady:

—*a patroness*, because to the sick who call on her patronage "she now shines radiantly as a sign of health, of healing, and of divine hope" (Pref);

—*a model*, because "to all who look up to her in prayer" she is "the model of perfect acceptance of [God's] will and of wholehearted conformity with Christ" (Pref).

To arrange Masses in honor of our Lady, health of the sick, and to ask her intercession for the recovery of health is to celebrate the unique importance of the history of salvation, which will be brought to its completion and perfection when, in the coming of Christ in glory, "the last enemy to be destroyed is death" (1 Corinthians 15:26), and the bodies of the just will rise in incorruption.

The texts of this Mass, except for the Preface, are those to be found in the Mass of the Blessed Virgin Mary, Health of the Sick, from the *Proprium missarum Ordinis Ministrantium infirmis*, Vatican Polyglot Press, 1974, pp. 14–15, 27–30.

Entrance Antiphon Cf. Psalm 35:3; Jonah 2:3

I am the Savior of my people.
Whatever their troubles I will answer their cry.

COLLECT

Grant, Lord God, that we, your servants,
may rejoice in unfailing health of mind and body,
and, through the glorious intercession of Blessed Mary ever-Virgin,
may we be set free from present sorrow
and come to enjoy eternal happiness.
Through our Lord Jesus Christ, your Son,
who lives and reigns with you in the unity of the Holy Spirit,
God, for ever and ever.

PRAYER OVER THE OFFERINGS

Look, O Lord, upon the prayers and offerings of your faithful,
presented in the commemoration of Blessed Mary, the Mother of God,
that they may be pleasing to you
and may confer on us your help and forgiveness.
Through Christ our Lord.

Preface P 44, page 131.

Communion Antiphon Psalm 118:14

The Lord, my strength and my song, has become my Savior.

PRAYER AFTER COMMUNION

Lord our God.
on this memorial of the Blessed Virgin Mary, the Mother of Jesus,
we have received with joyful hearts
the healing Sacrament
of the Body and Blood of your only Son;
may this Sacrament bring us blessings in this life
and in the world to come.
Through Christ our Lord.

45. THE BLESSED VIRGIN MARY, QUEEN OF PEACE

Because of her close personal connection with her Son, the "Prince of Peace" (Ent Ant, Isaiah 9:6; 1 Read, Isaiah 9:1-3, 5-6), our Lady has been increasingly venerated as "Queen of peace": in the calendars of particular Churches and some religious institutes there is a memorial of her as "Queen of peace." It is worth recalling that Benedict XV in 1917, while a terrible war was raging, ordered that the invocation "Queen of peace" should be added to the Litany of Loreto.

This Mass commemorates the cooperation of our Lady in the reconciliation or "peace" between God and the human family brought about by Christ:

—in *the mystery of the Incarnation:* the lowly handmaid of the Lord receives God's word from the Angel Gabriel and conceives in her virginal womb the Prince of Peace (cf. Pref; cf. Gos, Luke 1:26-38), who "has restored our peace, reconciling in himself earth with heaven" (Com Ant);

—in *the mystery of the Passion:* the faithful Mother stands "fearless beside the Cross as her Son sheds his Blood for our salvation and reconciles all things to himself in peace" (Pref);

—in *the mystery of Pentecost:* our Lady, the daughter of peace, joins "in prayer with the Apostles as she awaits . . . the Spirit of unity and peace, of love and joy" (Pref).

In celebrating the memorial of the Blessed Virgin Mary, Queen of Peace, the assembly of the faithful begs God that through her intercession he will grant to the Church and to the human family these favors:

—*the spirit of love:* "that we may live in peace as one family, united in love for one another" (Col); "bestow on us . . . the spirit of charity" (PC);

—*the gifts of unity and peace:* "bestow on your family the gifts of unity and peace" (PO); that "we may live in peace as one family" (Col); that "we may be effective in nurturing among all the peace that he has left us" (PC);

—*tranquility in our times:* "hear our earnest prayer; grant that our times may be tranquil" (Col).

The texts of this Mass, except for the Preface, are taken from the booklet *Proprio delle messe per le diocesi di Savona e Noli*, Tipografia Priamar, Savona, 1978, p. 17.

Entrance Antiphon Cf. Isaiah 9:6

A child is born for us,
a son is given to us,
and he shall be called "Prince of Peace."

COLLECT

Lord our God, you sent your only Son
to bring peace to our world.
Through the intercession
of Blessed Mary ever-Virgin,
hear our earnest prayer;
grant that our times may be tranquil,
so that we may live in peace as one family,
united in love for one another.
Through our Lord Jesus Christ, your Son,
who lives and reigns with you in the unity of the Holy Spirit,
God, for ever and ever.

PRAYER OVER THE OFFERINGS

Lord, as we lovingly venerate
Blessed Mary ever-Virgin, as Queen of Peace,
we offer you the sacrifice of reconciliation;
be pleased with our offering,
and bestow on your family
the gifts of unity and peace.
Through Christ our Lord.

Preface P 45, page 132.

Communion Antiphon

A virgin has given birth to one
who is truly God and truly human:
God has restored our peace,
reconciling in himself earth with heaven.

PRAYER AFTER COMMUNION

Bestow on us, we pray, O Lord, the spirit of charity,
on this memorial of Our Lady, Queen of Peace,
so that, refreshed by the Body and Blood of your Only
Begotten Son,
we may be effective in nurturing among all
the peace that he has left us.
Who lives and reigns for ever and ever.

46. THE BLESSED VIRGIN MARY, GATE OF HEAVEN

The final formulary in this collection of Masses of the Blessed Virgin Mary celebrates the Mother of God as she lovingly accompanies God's people on their pilgrimage to their true home in heaven.

The eschatological sense proper to the celebration of the Eucharist is central to this Mass: the assembly of the faithful contemplates "the holy city, the new Jerusalem, . . . arrayed like a bride for her husband," and hears the voice of the Lord from the heavenly throne, saying: "Behold, I make all things new" (1 Read, Revelation 21:1-5a). This future state of the Church has already been realized in our Lady, virgin and bride, in all her beauty, without stain or wrinkle (cf. Ephesians 5:27). The faithful joyfully go up "to the house of the Lord," where they will praise his name for ever (cf. Resp, Psalm 122:1-2, 3-4, 8-9). They are to stay watchful in order to go out to meet the Bridegroom with lighted lamps, so that when the door is opened they may be worthy of admission (cf. Gos, Matthew 25:1-13).

This Mass primarily celebrates Christ the Lord, whom his loving Father has made "the gateway to salvation and life" (Col; cf. John 10:7): Jesus, "who . . . opens the door of forgiveness" (Pref), through whom the gate of God's city in heaven has been thrown open to us (cf. Col).

The metaphors of "door" or "entrance" or "gate" or "threshold" have been applied from patristic times to our Lady to express her function as the second Eve, to express her virginal motherhood or her intercession for the faithful.

In this formulary our Lady is celebrated as:

—*the sinless Eve*, who has overcome the pride of the first woman by humility, Eve's disbelief by faith, reopening what had been closed: "She is the humble Virgin, whose faith opened the gate of eternal life, closed by the disbelief of Eve" (Pref); "the gates of paradise, closed by Eve, were reopened by you, O Virgin Mary" (*All*);

—*the Virgin Mother of Christ:* through her motherhood Mary is "the very gate of life," because from her "the Savior of the world came among us, Jesus Christ our Lord" (PO); the "resplendent gate of light," through whom "there came to shine on us Christ, the light of the world" (Com Ant); the "Maiden-Mother, bearing the Word of God, . . . the gate of paradise," who "in bringing God into the world" has "unlocked for us the gate of heaven" (Ent Ant);

—*the prayerful voice of intercession* (cf. Pref): the Church does not doubt that "through the Blessed Virgin Mary, who brought our Savior into the world, [God's] gifts of grace may come down on us and the gate of heaven may be opened to receive us into the joy of [God's] Kingdom" (PC).

Entrance Antiphon

Maiden-Mother, bearing the Word of God,
you are the gate of paradise;
in bringing God into the world
you have unlocked for us the gate of heaven.

COLLECT

Lord our God, in your goodness
you have made your Son
the gateway to salvation and life;
grant that, as we follow the example
of the Blessed Virgin Mary,
we may remain faithful in the love of Christ
and so pass safely through the gate
of your city in heaven.
Through our Lord Jesus Christ, your Son,
who lives and reigns with you in the unity of the Holy Spirit,
God, for ever and ever.

PRAYER OVER THE OFFERINGS

Lord, we offer to the glory of your name
the Sacrament of unity and peace
as we honor the memory of the glorious Virgin Mary,
the very gate of life,
through whom the Savior of the world came among us,
Jesus Christ our Lord.
Who lives and reigns for ever and ever.

Preface P 46, page 133.

Communion Antiphon

**Blessed are you, Virgin Mary, resplendent gate of light;
through you there came to shine on us Christ, the light of the world.**

PRAYER AFTER COMMUNION

**Refreshed, Lord God, by this joyous Sacrament,
we pray that through the Blessed Virgin Mary,
who brought our Savior into the world,
your gifts of grace may come down on us
and the gate of heaven may be opened to receive us
into the joy of your Kingdom.
Through Christ our Lord.**

ALPHABETICAL INDEX OF MASSES

ALPHABETICAL INDEX OF PREFACES